The River Behind The Hill

A Celebration of Australian Fly Fishing

The River Behind The Hill

A Celebration of Australian Fly Fishing

PHILIP WEIGALL

NEW HOLLAND

First published in Australia in 1999 by
New Holland Publishers (Australia) Pty Ltd
Sydney • Auckland • London • Cape Town

14 Aquatic Drive Frenchs Forest NSW 2086 Australia
218 Lake Road Northcote Auckland New Zealand
24 Nutford Place London W1H 6DQ United Kingdom
80 McKenzie Street Cape Town 8001 South Africa

Copyright © 1999 in text: Philip Weigall
Copyright © 1999 in maps: Annette Busse, Colin Wynter Seton
Copyright © 1999 in illustration: Mark Thacker
Copyright © 1999 in photographs: as credited below
Copyright © 1999 New Holland Publishers (Australia) Pty Ltd

National Library of Australia Cataloguing-in-Publication Data:

Weigall, Philip.
The River Behind the Hill: A celebration of Australian flyfishing

Includes index.
ISBN 1 86436 518 8

1. Weigall, Philip. 2. Fly fishing–Australia. I. Title

799.1240994

Publishing General Manager: Jane Hazell
Publisher: Averill Chase
Commissioning Editor: Anouska Good
Editors: Howard Gelman, Rick Keam
Designer: Mark Thacker, Big Cat Design
Reproduction: South China Printing Co. (1988) Ltd.
Separation: Colour Symphony Pte Ltd.
Printed in Hong Kong by South China Printing

Photographic Acknowledgements

Photographic positions: t–top; b–bottom; l–left; r–right
Jane Gardner: fishing notes, pp. 2 8–9, 10, 12, 14, 19, 24, 26, 32, 43, 56, 57, 59, 60, 62, 62t,
67b, 70, 79, 80, 91, 9,6, 99, 106, 108, 114, 122, 133, 137, 140; *courtesy of* **Peter Luck:** p. 6; **P. Murray:**
p. 29; **David Roche:** pp. 16, 33, 40t, 60t, 68t, 72, 75, 91b, 96t, 110t, 118, 129b, 133b, 136tr; **R. D. Sloane/
Tas-Trout Publications:** pp. 16, 23, 31, 35, 37, 55r, 76, 78, 89, 100, 115, 120, 125, 146; **Mark Thacker:**
pp. 3, 15, 22, 28, 36, 44, 55bl, 58, 64b, 67t, 83, 88b, 104t, 126b, 127, 128b, 136br, 160; **Mark Weigall:**
pp. 17, 40, 82, 103, 109, 110b; **Philip Weigall:** pp. 5, 18, 20, 21, 30, 34, 38, 39, 41, 48, 49, 50, 51,
54, 65, 66, 68b, 73, 74, 77, 81, 84, 86, 88t, 90, 92, 94, 97, 98, 102, 104b, 111, 112, 113,
116, 117, 119, 124, 126t, 128t, 130, 132, 134, 135, 138, 139, 141, 142.

To Jane

Acknowledgements

The River Behind the Hill is far from a solo effort. To begin with, I owe a lot to the generous contributions of those who provided so much for this book for no reward other than my gratitude:

• My partner, Jane Gardner, who not only helped immensely with refining the manuscript, but who also contributed many of her beautifully composed transparencies.

• Rob Sloane, who, unbidden, offered the use of slides from a sizeable chunk of his rich library

• My brother Mark, who also passed me a big box of his best pics (not quite as neatly filed as Rob's) and said 'go for your life'.

The professionals who worked on the book were an author's delight. My special thanks go to:

• Howard Gelman, the project coordinator at New Holland. Howard did a great job organising a structurally complex book under the inevitably tight time constraints, while also providing welcome editorial input. All this at the same time as having to master 'fly fishing-ese'!

• Anouska Good, New Holland's commissioning editor, who showed nothing but infectious enthusiasm for the whole project from the start, and who has provided continuous and heartfelt support at every stage since.

• Rick Keam, whose editing skills go beyond mere grammar to include a rare sense of order, place and perspective; and a rare depth of knowledge about all things fly fishing related. Rick is another who put in a lot more effort than could reasonably be expected.

• Mark Thacker from Big Cat Design, who became so committed to the project that he drove 1000 kilometres from Sydney to Windy Hill (our home) during his own holiday time to spend a few days with Jane and I perfecting the photographic content and design. We learned a lot from Mark and he learned a bit from us, including the fact that even eight pound tippet is not necessarily enough to stop an eight pound rainbow!

Many people will recognise Peter Luck for his pre-eminence as a journalist and television presenter, but few will know of his passion for fly fishing. Peter's foreword will delight all who love the sport, and perhaps it may help to convert a few who presently do not! There could be no better introduction to this book, and my sincere thanks to Peter for his involvement.

Foreword

Fly fishing must be one of the most exclusive pastimes on earth. In fact, I think in my whole life I've met more Prime Ministers than I have fly fishermen ... half a dozen of the former, maybe five of the latter. Over the years I've struck up conversations with more people who have jumped out of aeroplanes, more people who have sailed in the Sydney–Hobart race, more who have trekked through Nepal. I've met more men who've

wielded the willow in a test cricket match than have wafted a split cane over their shoulder in a trout stream, certainly more women who've drifted a backhand over the net at Wimbledon than have tried to make a Royal Coachmen alight without a splash on a millpond. So why is it that so many fascinating books, such as this one, have been written about such an arcane and little practised art? Walton, Farson, Haig-Brown, Schwiebert, Ritz, Pawson, Hole are just some of the many who've felt they needed to put it all into words.

And it says something about the romantic mystique of the whole pursuit that there are apparently tens of thousands of others who want to be told about fly fishing, read about it, or watch it on television—even if they never actually get that privileged chance to wet a line or, even more exclusively, tie the fly. I've only encountered three human beings who practise that craft and, come to think of it, I've met more Governors-General than that!

Indeed, it actually was a Prime Minister, Malcolm Fraser, who unwittingly introduced me to the beguiling sport/art (spart?) of fly fishing. More than three decades ago Big Mal, bless his heart, told my dear friend Richard Carleton about a wonderful river that he fished in the Brindabella range west of Canberra.

Richard and I went there together and were instantly transported by the ravishing beauty of the place and its flora and fauna. We both eventually managed to secure shares of that Shangri La. Indeed, Richard was so overwhelmed by it he bought the old Brindabella station. The magical valley has been part of our lives for the past 30 years. From their earliest days our children have grown up with the ethos of that bush, the river, and fishing. 'I think you've caught a snag,' I once said to my son Anthony as he wrestled with a rod at the age of five or so. 'What do snags eat?' he cried out excitedly.

In this spellbinding, sparkling, enchanted river and wild countryside trout abound, rainbows and browns—but oh, aren't they contrary critters? There is only one rule with trout: 'There are no rules.' Every day brings some revelation. Just when you thought you had everything 'sussed' out something happens to shatter your complacency. Trout grow to the size of their respective streams and in 80 years of records, the largest fish caught in ours has been around seven pounds. In 30 years, the largest I've ever landed has been around four pounds and sometimes I might go two or three years seeing only one or two fish as large as that. And yet—just to give you an idea of how elusive and contradictory these fish are—during my last sortie, in the middle of a drought with the river very low, I saw in a single day maybe two or three hundred fish of five pounds or more sometimes schooling in frenzied groups of twenty or so.

The point is, I would have laid good money in the past half century that the entire river contained only a few large fish. So where do they go…where do they come from…and why do they tease and tantalise us thus? Of course, the answer is that this is part of the joy of it all. Angler's hell, after all, is sitting on a beautiful river bank somewhere in the Cosmos throughout eternity pulling out a big fish on every cast—the challenge has gone. And maybe this is why trout fishing is surrounded by such an ambience of art and literature. As we sit and ponder and even curse the elusiveness of fish, there is so much time for the Muse to strike…time to write the music and poetry that has been inspired by such a seemingly mundane thing as swinging a stick over your head. There is time to draw the drawings and paint the paintings and write the books, such as this. And there is even time—if you are fatally attracted by the bug and have risen to the lure—yes, even time to tie your own flies and ponder whether there is any more satisfying achievement in the Cosmos.

PETER LUCK

…But a man's what his spirit knows;

And what I have known for a truth, now as in youth

Is one clear river, coming down cold from the snows.

DOUGLAS STEWART, 'THE RIVER'

Contents

CHAPTER ONE

The Source

When I first started trout fishing, the local river lay enticingly over the back of a single large, bald hill. Thirty seasons on, the stream nearest to my home is similarly concealed. Though I catch myself dreaming of the day when I can watch cruising trout from my very window, something always beckons about water just out of reach. On the river behind the hill, deep beneath the blackwood shade on a secret bend, the largest fish never stops rising.

To identify how fly fishing came to take such a hold on my life, I have to go back to my earliest explorations with a rod. My first fish was an eel

right: Success near Mt Buller, after some 30 years.

from the Yarra River, caught with a worm suspended from a primitive bamboo pole. I was just three. Though remembering little else before my fifth birthday, I can recall everything to do with the capture of that slimy, extraordinary creature. The dew dripping off the tea-tree bushes that crowded dark against the edge of the river. The cold clammy touch of the worms that tried to hide among the soil in Uncle John's yellow bucket. His kind hands helping me to hold the rod the right way, and to assist against the mysterious strong pulls of something unseen.

Once I had landed the writhing eel, Uncle John humanely dispatched it with all necessary force, half severing its head with his knife. I cannot remember feeling either pity or thrill in its death: just a half-hearted curiosity. Even at three years of age, all the excitement was in the capture, not the killing. There was something almost miraculous about being able to extract a living thing from a world as utterly foreign as the silty, cold depths of the Yarra River.

In any case, it appears that I lacked a solid grasp of the notion of mortality, because I decided to keep the mutilated eel as a pet. This seemed perfectly sensible to me at the time, and was accepted with good humour by my parents and uncle. No doubt they were confident that I would soon grow tired of carting around something limp, lifeless and increasingly smelly. Their confidence was misplaced, and a day later my pet had to be finally 'liberated' (back into the river, I was told) while I slept.

My next memorable fish was a redfin, caught under the bridge at Bonnie Doon on Lake Eildon. All of fifteen centimetres, it was notable for being caught without any aid from an adult. The rest of the family were picnicking some distance down the shore when I cast, hooked and landed my prize.

below: A basic bait fishing rod and reel from the early days.

As significant as the eel and the redfin were, neither compete with my first trout. Having recently moved to the foothills of Mount Buller, and being surrounded by trout streams, Dad had sensibly decided to learn trout fishing in earnest. He generously allowed six-year-old Philip to join him, at least some of the time, and was sufficiently new to it all that we were able to make some discoveries together. The rare experience of being a participant and co-discoverer with an adult, rather than being only a pupil, may have helped make fishing so appealing so early in my life.

above: The first fly I ever tied, the Red Tag. Still a favourite.

Most of our adventures took place on the Delatite River, which flowed on the far side of the hill in front of our house. Being only a mile or so distant, it was by far the closest decent-sized stream. Small trout also swam in the little creek that was audible from our verandah, but even as a second grader I could distinguish between this toy stream and the much more serious and promising depths of the river.

We always seemed to go fishing late in the afternoon, and the headlights on our EH Holden were usually required for the drive home. I cannot remember if this time of day was chosen for angling reasons or simply because it fitted in after work and school commitments. When my first trout plays like a short film in my head, I know that the lighting is not dim because of the distance of time, but because the shadows were already long when we walked from the car across Klingsporn's paddock to the river.

Although a thick belt of willow, blackberry and tea-tree enclosed much of the river, there was a section where a bend swung in toward us against a steep hill. Here shallow soil, exposure to direct sunlight and constant stock traffic had kept the bank bare of all vegetation except moss and tufts of hardy grass. This easy access was made doubly attractive by the large pool that formed at the apex of the bend. We were both at the stage in trout fishing where we believed that the biggest pools promised the most, and this one was an obvious target.

above: A small, beautifully marked brown trout typical of the Otway streams.

I sat on a cool patch of sand atop a point where the bank dropped steeply into dark water, and carefully threaded a worm to my hook. The mysterious pool looked all the more fishy now that the sharp rays of sun had retreated to the highest ridges. Bush noises from the forest across the river mixed with the aimless calls of cattle in the paddock. I heard a splash from upriver, too far away to identify the cause. Was it a platypus or water rat…or better?

In all this observation of the surroundings, I had forgotten to cast. It took a conscious effort to refocus on the river and a likely place for my bait. The deep water right below seemed appealing, but I gazed over the whole area in case there was something better. I was too young and too inexperienced to really know what I was looking for, so I can't really explain why I did what I did, but I was to be rewarded for my trouble.

On the far bank was an extensive sandy shallow. The water was very clear, and in the flat twilight it was surprisingly easy to see the rocks and sticks that punctuated the sand. And there was something else: a trout. I don't recall which of us saw it first, but I'm sure we were equally amazed to actually see a trout swimming free in the water. Nor do I know who cast my rod, though I remember seeing the plop where my sinker landed, and knowing that it marked where the worm lay on the sand. The trout, a couple of rod lengths away, showed no response for a second or two but then swam deliberately across the pale stream bed to the vicinity of my invisible bait. It searched around and the next moment I felt a firm tug on the line.

above: Reliving the thrill of that first seriously big trout. Teenager Rob Spicer (right), then relatively new to fly fishing, shows me his trophy, caught on a dry.

above: Autumn fog on the Mitta, an important river all through my fly fishing life.

After the blurry commotion that followed, my nine-inch prize (two short of the legal limit) lay on the bank beside me. Recognising that the significance of the occasion outweighed mere matters of law, Dad ventured that I could keep it, but with some reluctance I chose the 'adult' approach and let it go.

Eventually, a new work posting for Dad drew us away from the mountains. The dry and largely treeless expanse of our new home in the southern Barrabool Hills offered nothing in the way of familiar trout water. The horizontal blue-grey smudge of the Otway Ranges provided the closest surrogate for the forested mountains and rubble-bottomed streams of the Buller region. Though smaller in every respect, the Otways felt like home. There was no happier time at that point in my life than a trip to these hills and the small trout streams enfolded within them.

My first fly-caught trout was taken from a small Otway creek rejoicing in the name of the Grey River. I was camped on its banks with my longest serving fishing companion outside immediate family, David Julian. At this stage I primarily fished spinner and bait, but had begun to dabble in fly fishing. I was unable then, as now, to distract David from his post-lunch afternoon nap. So I headed downstream to entertain myself for an hour or so, deciding for some reason to take the fly rod. I had a low regard for my fly fishing skill at that time, so I can only guess that I did this to justify the bother of carting it through the scrub to our campsite in the first place.

I pushed my way a few hundred metres down the valley through the tree ferns and fallen beech logs, keeping a respectful distance from the water, and rejoined the creek at a point where a small cascade bubbled into a circular pool. I liked this feature, recalling several occasions when a spinner or mudeye cast in right under the cascade had produced a strike from a trout. It seemed sensible to adopt the same strategy with my fly, and after a few uneasy false casts, I was delighted when my Royal Coachman landed right in the middle of the turbulence. My delight was immediately replaced with puzzlement as the Royal sank like a stone in the white water. I knew that a dry fly was supposed to float, and that the cue to strike was the sight of a trout actually sucking it off the surface. Unsure of what to do under these different circumstances, I lifted the rod in preparation to cast again. Yank!

above: Summer on the middle reaches of the Delatite River.

The rod tip pulled away from me, and to my utter amazement a brown trout was dancing about on the end of my line. Not a bad one either—eleven inches—so it would have been 'legal' even before the then recent abolition of limits. Popping the trout in my bag I moved upstream, confident for the first time that I could catch one of these fish on a fly, though bemused about the actual process.

The next pool was hardly a pool at all, more a rock hole, but its importance was transformed when I saw a fish feed from the surface right in the middle. From my hiding place behind a sandstone boulder, all I had to do to present the fly to the required area

was to flick the rod tip. It landed amid some loops of leader, then flopped forlornly on its side and looked in danger of sinking, even in the calm water. But before this could happen the white wings disappeared in the rings of a rise! Providentially, the fact that I was too stunned to react instantly ensured that the trout had properly taken the fly before I managed to strike. Measuring eight inches on my fishing bag ruler, this one was definitely too small to keep. It didn't matter: my second ever trout on the fly had actually been caught 'properly', if a little untidily.

One more trout grabbed the Royal Coachman on the way back to camp, but this time I was too ready and struck before the fish had time to close its mouth. Never mind, I thought, this fly fishing actually works. My first *wet fly* trout, a big one, came not long after on the Barwon River. Once again a fair amount of luck was involved. Unsure of exactly what I was meant to do, I had fed line downstream and was letting the Black and Red Matuka swing in the current at the tail of a pool. The boil and pull of a strong trout was totally unexpected, but everything held together and I grassed an honest two pounder, one of my best trout ever at the time and by far the best on a fly.

above: Late May rainbow, from Hepburn Lagoon, near my home in the central highlands of Victoria.

opposite: Jane, my partner, casting to rises in the ripple at Upper Coliban Reservoir, scene of some of my earliest stillwater success with the fly.

Those three fly-caught trout remain as sharp in my mind now as they did when their cool slickness writhed in my hands. I remember others with the same vividness, though forgetting exactly where they fell in the chronology of my early fly fishing life. Some I recall for the sting of disappointment when large trout that I wanted so badly in my bag were lost. There was the five-pounder on the Bundarra River, so beaten that it wallowed on its side before the hook pulled out, under less force than had been applied in the entire ten minutes beforehand. If you have ever tried to recapture a fleeing escapee, even a tired one half-stranded in the shallows, you will appreciate my desperate grasps at my trophy as it squirmed inevitably toward the safety of deep water. The panicked swipe with the net on a frosty Mitta morning that left a monstrous fish momentarily hanging on the outside of the mesh before something broke and it crashed back into the river and away. But unlike some other disappointments in life, losses of large trout in fly fishing are a spur to try harder. I do not recall the slightest inclination to give up after losing big fish—only an increased desire to succeed next time.

And there are plenty of kinder memories. The miracle of the first Cairn Curran smelter, more than five pounds of silver that suddenly decided to grab my Hamill's Killer after dozens of trout had seemingly ignored it. Not to mention a period of prolific success nymphing the Howqua River and Jim Crow Creek to the point where, for a while, I used nothing else wherever I fished.

below: Felt-soled wading boots are essential for safe progress among the slippery rubble that lines many mountain streams.

Memories are, of course, one of the great gifts all fly fishers receive. Sometimes they have a habit of blending with the present, as if to remind us of the significance of earlier days. Not long ago, Dad told me that he was planning a day's fishing with an old school master of mine, John Bedggood. I didn't hesitate to accept the invitation to join them. Being late May the fishing around my home was winding down, but that was no deterrent. Besides my enjoyment of John's company, he holds special rank as one of the first fly fishers I knew, and the person who taught me to tie flies. The last honour is a somewhat dubious one because to this day I am a mediocre to poor fly-tier. I may well have peaked under John's tuition at the age of twelve! But I am forever grateful for those fly-tying classes, not so much for the teaching, but for keeping alive my angling dreams during school days when real fishing opportunities were unbearably far apart.

The day out with John and Dad was an unusually warm one for late autumn. With the light breeze, humid air and meringue clouds that sat around doing nothing, you would normally pick it as a great fishing day. However, it came after a fortnight of miserably grey and wintry weather. Such days seem to take nature by surprise. Everything appears a little stunned, like a late night party goer who has rashly opened the blinds on a sunny morning.

Though it was pleasant to be out, the action was a trifle slow and there was plenty of time for talk, mainly about things related to fishing. I have met John several times since school days. What made this occasion different was that we were actually fishing. Having always known that he fly fished, for the first time I was watching him do it. As he poked around in his fly box, I could see the flies he tied with the same fingers that patiently demonstrated in a draughty classroom a quarter-century earlier.

above: Discovering that the Red Tag still works on the Mitta River.

above: Waiting for the evening rise on the Delatite River. The summit of Mt Buller is just visible on the extreme left. We lived near the base of Mt Timbertop, the next peak to the right.

I sat on some dry rushes waiting for the odd 'oncer' out in the middle of the lake to become something more regular and closer. Naturally, with a part of my own fly fishing history casting away on the other shore, I found myself thinking back. Maybe it was the same for my teacher, because when we stopped for a hot drink the conversation turned without effort to our respective beginnings with the fly.

I was telling John about my maiden trout on a fly, the one from the Grey River, when I suddenly realised that it fell to a creation tied in his very classroom. The Royal Coachman was a step up in difficulty from the beginner's Red Tag because of the addition of a fiddly wing. I remember assuming that this extra complexity would confer superior fish-catching ability: it was many more years before I learned that complication did not necessarily equal more trout.

And then, for just a moment, I saw my twelve-year-old self with total clarity. The novice flyfisher, dressed in school uniform without a rod or river in sight. All the uncertainty, coupled with an urge to learn as much as possible as quickly as possible. And above all, a desire simply to go fishing. Not just to the places I had been before, but to the new and unknown waters that lay ahead.

Getting Started

If possible, get help from an experienced fly fishing friend, fly club member or professional instructor who has the patience to teach you to cast. There are some 'naturals' who manage to teach themselves, but there are many other self-taught casters who have developed bad habits that are difficult to break.

Once you get on top of casting, you can devote attention to other things, and both your learning curve and enjoyment will skyrocket. I must warn you, though, that you'll spend the rest of your life trying to figure out some of the finer points of the sport!

Be prepared to show some dedication. Fly fishing is not something for a few days a year.

Concentrate your early efforts on fast mountain streams with high trout populations, like those of northeast Victoria, Tasmania and the Snowy Mountains area of New South Wales. The turbulent water will help mask your mistakes, and the trout have to make quick decisions as your fly flashes past, meaning fly selection is less critical.

Use buoyant, easy-to-see dry flies like the Royal Wulff and Red Tag. If that doesn't work, try a weighted brown nymph one metre under a strike indicator (a small piece of greasy wool straight off a fence is ideal).

CHAPTER TWO

The Ant Feeder

On trout water a seat is where you find it. An island stump in a marshy bay, or a mossy log by a rainforest stream. After hours on foot, it doesn't matter if it isn't in the Chesterfield class. And of course there is always the view.

Mostly I fish hard, so when I sit down there's usually a reason. The best of these is the contented 'I've caught a lot of fish/caught a big fish' seat. Grin a little smugly, stretch that sore rod arm (even if it really isn't that sore), and enjoy the scenery.

The worst is the frustrated/exhausted seat, the one where you slump down and stretch your rod arm, because it is actually sore from all that fruitless casting. Why can't I polaroid any trout? Where the heck are the duns? How I wish the wind would drop twenty or thirty knots.

A couple of years ago, I took a seat on the banks of a remote section of the upper Swampy Plains River. If ever there was a river behind a hill, it is the upper Swampy. Near enough to two vertical kilometres of the Main Range, culminating in Australia's tallest peak, shadow its forested course. Less familiar and famous than the blue-ribbon tailwater below Khancoban, this precipitous and impossibly clear stream has its own charms. Old timers talk of the days before the Snowy Scheme diverted water from the river, when it flowed with awesome strength and held perhaps the finest river rainbows in Australia. Where the river has gouged through raw rock, it is still possible to make out the dark stain that reflects the old height. Little grows beneath this mark. Even the wizened tea-tree does not creep below it, seemingly fearful that the old flows might one day return.

No, the upper Swampy is not the fishery it once was. But in its reduced state it is still an impressive stretch of river, and while the monster rainbows seem all but extinct, more modest specimens sway like tendrils of mist in the fastest water. Regulation high country browns are plentiful.

On this day my break was an enforced one. The leader had become frayed and short, and tying a nail knot is preferably a job to be done while seated. Even so, I enjoyed taking the weight off my feet. In the muggy afternoon shade, the dry rocks felt cool and smooth, giving relief to sweating limbs. The fishing had been steady; possibly a little slower in the last stretch of water. Two solid hours hop-scotching up the river gorge warranted a rest, new leader requirements or not. My brother Mark had elected to walk down river and fish back up toward our camp, and I wondered how he was faring on the untried water down there.

With a little wriggling I found a comfortable position among the pebbles and rocks on the gravel bar, leaned back against a sword-grass tussock and breathed in the sight of forested slopes climbing up at almost impossible angles. On the near perpendicular cliff faces scraggly gums had somehow found footholds on the tiniest ledges. I wondered absently how a seed could find its way to such a remote perch, and how the hard granite rock provided any sustenance for growth.

Here, away from the rapids, the river did not roar and thunder. Instead it hissed and gurgled. Viewed from a low angle under a heavy grey sky, the constancy of the little

above: A handy tool for fly fishers in a range of situations, binoculars can be especially useful when scouting lakes for subtle riseforms the naked eye might miss.

whirlpools and ripples on the river's surface made the flow seem almost static. Then the passage of solitary bubbles and debris would break the momentary illusion, and tell that a relentless flow of water continued to pass this spot. Day and night, month after month, century after century, the river water made its way toward the distant Southern Ocean.

Recharged, and with a brand new leader, I rose to my feet. Once more in my perceptions the river became foremost a residence for trout. The clear water was slick and cold, with holding lies behind boulders, in current seams, pools, runs and rapids. Though the sun remained hidden behind cloud, the summer warmth was trapped in this valley, and the possibility of insects drifting down the river was strong: more likely than if the sunlight were streaming down. Insects of these kinds like life warm and humid, or at least such weather seems to result in plenty of them becoming trapped in the morass of the river's surface film. A speck lodged in my eye. I blinked in irritation, and instinctively rubbed the offended spot. There was relief as the piece of grit caught on my fingertip.

above: Pre-thunderstorm ant feeder from an upper Murray River eddy.

above: Lindsay Waters with an inshore ant feeder from Dee Lagoon.

opposite: Likely ant water on the Buffalo River.

Glancing at the annoying article, I found it was an ant. A flying ant. I forgot about my sore eye and started looking for more. How many were in the air? Even more important, how many on the water?

It is said that of all prey, trout find ants the most enticing. The theory is that ants have a sweet tangy taste due to their formic acid content and trout find this taste irresistible. Fly fishers have a bad habit of endowing trout with human features such as finding a certain taste irresistible, so I don't know how much credence should be given to this. I will say that whatever the reason—and maybe it *is* the nice taste—trout feed on ants with a vigour few other insects can activate.

As with most hatches and falls, there is usually a short lull between the appearance of the first flying ants and the onset of serious feeding by the trout. While I waited expectantly on the Swampy, my mind drifted back to encounters with ants from summers past. Some recollections sparked a sense of optimism, like an eerily wonderful afternoon on the middle reaches of the Jamieson, backlit by a monstrous thunderhead racked by lightning. The trout rose by the dozen in the only pool I had time to fish, and in the tail alone I landed seven. But then there were sessions like the one at Dee Lagoon with Rob Sloane and Mark.

The day in question was overcast, with veils of thin drizzle periodically inching across the lake in the almost windless conditions. Earlier in the week, balmy weather had produced good falls of gum beetles from the steep forested shores, and we had enjoyed exciting though demanding fishing to speeding rainbows and sullen browns. Such sport seemed unlikely this day, and we had seen no more than the odd unpredictable rise across acres of the lake's oily surface. Nevertheless, we boarded Rob's boat.

above: A muggy late afternoon on the Indi River—fingers crossed for a flying ant fall.

At first we saw nothing to boost our hopes. Then we rounded a headland into a concealed bay. Two schools of rainbow trout, numbering perhaps ten fish each, were lazily porpoising like synchronised dolphins. Some of them were clearly bigger than two kilos, a couple closer to three. The mood in the boat changed instantly. One moment we were going through the motions, the next we were fishing. I didn't have to ask to know what the others were thinking. How could we miss?

The first imperative was to look at the water for the abundant food source that was creating this frenzy. But that's when the first problem arose: there wasn't anything there! What was going on? Could it be that the insects creating the rises, still fifty metres way, were absent on our patch of water? It was agreed that that must be it.

Then came another suggestion. Maybe the fish weren't rising at all but taking emergers just under the surface, like midges perhaps. Watching all those broad backs cutting meticulously through the surface made us all the more impatient for action. In the absence of hard evidence, we decided to persist with our small generalist patterns, using Red Tags for the surface and a little wet beetle for just below.

above: A flying ant tied by David Dodd.

We failed that afternoon. Such was the apathy of the trout to our flies, or rather their complete indifference, that perfect presentations right in the path of any cruising fish were rejected. Utterly. Neither the slightest deviation nor flicker of recognition could be cajoled from those single-minded rainbows.

It is easy to be philosophical about fishless days when the conditions are rotten and there's not a fish to be seen. It's another matter when the trout are feeding hard within comfortable casting distance. We scanned the surface once more in the fading light, frantically searching for a clue. And there it was, almost invisible. Millions of tiny black ants, so tiny that two could have hidden behind a single match-head. How, we wondered, could such puny prey be worth a large rainbow's while?

As the last daylight was swallowed by night, the mystery was solved. A big rainbow hit Mark's Sunset Fly, and after several reel-screeching runs the fish was landed. The trout was earmarked for a barbeque back at the cabin, so he cleaned it. In its stomach was a fistful of thousands of the tiny ants, looking like a mound of black, damp sawdust. As minute as they were, the ants had been present in such quantities that even a big trout could fill its belly. I doubt if there was ever a fly hook small enough to imitate those ants, and regular ant patterns were ignored. I wonder still if there is anything we could have tried that would have brought those trout undone.

But back to the Swampy Plains River, where the flying ants were clumsily landing on the water with increasing frequency. Whether this behaviour was by confused design or accident, they were immediately doomed. Their floppy oversized wings stuck fast, and they wriggled or lay drowned in the surface film.

The ant quantity must eventually have hit some magical number and the trout responded in unison. At once the glide before me was pocked with determined sips and slurps. Ant feeders are not inclined toward caution. To the unseasoned, such a rise would appear certain to produce fantastic results. Experiences such as the Dee Lagoon episode, however, suggested otherwise. Although the ants were of imitable size, perhaps hook size 16 or 18, it was clear that catching these trout would be far from a pushover.

I considered the contradictory possibility that masses of insects on the water are not always a guarantee of fly fishing nirvana. The trout can choose from a multitude of naturals. Even with plenty of fish working there are numerous surviving insects that float by unscathed, for the trout are not quick enough to catch every one. So if some naturals are being ignored, it certainly stacks the odds against your artificial being accepted.

Another hurdle is selectivity. Generally trout are far more opportunistic in their feeding than many of us will accept, and trout stomachs frequently contain a diverse range of food. But there are occasions when there is such a surfeit of one food type that the fish will feed selectively on it to the exclusion of all else. It seems that under such conditions minority organisms fail to register in their awareness, which is totally dominated by the image of the super-abundant insect. It is as if their primitive brains recognise the value of pursuing the most prolific food and eliminate any distractions, so gaining maximum energy advantage from the opportunity presented. This dooms the angler to failure if he cannot present a fly that will either trigger that dormant part of the brain concerned with seeking food other than 'Insect X', or else mimic the shape, colour and behaviour of Insect X so closely that it is accepted as such. Well, that's what the theory says anyway.

below: Peter Murray at work on the Indi during one of the best autumn ant falls I can remember.

The final irritation is less common, but it does happen. Because there is so much to eat, the fish basically fill up and stop feeding very quickly, leaving all the extra beetles or minnows or whatever to go to waste. Trout that are not feeding are very difficult to catch.

A heavy rise doesn't always turn out to be the most *productive* situation for a fly fisher, but there are few spectacles we enjoy more. A textbook angler beside me on the Swampy might have overcome the screaming urge to cast straight away. Not me. In an initial burst of impatience, I covered one of the nearer fish four or five times with the large Royal Wulff already tied to the new leader.

An hour or so ago it had been as good a dry as any, bringing regular takes in the fast water at least, and confirming its standing as one of the better generic dry flies. Now it was ignored, and I wasn't really surprised. With a steady stream of ants drifting down the river, it seemed that the normal 'try anything food-like' tendencies of the trout had been replaced by 'try anything ant-like'. This meant a low-floating body and a clear halo of wings draped on the surface. The well-hackled Wulff was a fly still shimmering in the outside world, not trapped at the boundary of air and water.

If I persisted long enough, especially in fast water, it could be that the attractive properties of this classic pattern would catch the eye of a trout sufficiently to draw it from the obvious feast. That had happened a few times on trips gone by. But looking at the situation analytically, I had to come up with something that was closer to a real ant in terms of its position in the surface film and its size.

With ants now carpeting the river like tiny leaves, the old veterans from the most shadowy lies joined in the rise. On this and many similar waters these outsized trout are hardly ever seen by anglers. Once or twice a year one might fall at night to an old farmer's set line. Rarer still is their capture at night by a fly fisher on a big wet fly or noisy dry. On those unique occasions when a hook-up actually happens, the encounter usually ends in a broken tippet without the fish ever being sighted. The shaking angler is left to ask the question that is never answered: how big was that?

above: On the upper Swampy and many similar mountain rivers, it takes an abundance of food like flying ants to bring a trout like this to the surface in daylight.

These trout are extremely rare—perhaps no more than one fish in every few hundred adults on a freestone river like the upper Swampy. Their prosperity is cause for admiration. Somehow these exceptional fish have learned to feed more efficiently, perhaps even learning to capitalise on a unique food source, and this along with genetics may explain their unusual growth rate or their ability to outlive their brethren.

As the surface activity built toward a serious rise, such curious speculation about the reasons for big fish was far from my mind. The glide before me was already rippled by the piercing snouts of several trout, at least a couple of which looked to be over a kilo: fine fish in this river where the honest 'average' is lucky to be a third that weight. But it was at least one, perhaps two, trout on the opposite bank that caused me to stop casting for a minute and squint past the rises in the main current.

The far bank was virtually a cliff, its bare rock punctuated by clumps of grass and desperately clinging trees. The slope was obviously unstable, and halfway along the glide a caravan-sized boulder had toppled into the river. The jagged obstruction jutted into the current like a black iceberg, causing a lazy eddy to form on its lee side. Within this small backwater, it was just possible to see a few trapped objects like twigs and bubbles circling slowly. When I looked really hard, I could see the soft, silent rings of feeding trout.

It was the location of these rises that first aroused my suspicion that they might belong to out-of-the-ordinary fish. Giant trout are fair game for all sorts of theories about where they live, when they feed and how they can be caught. Fair game because they are so rare that there's not much chance of actually disproving a given theory with some cold-blooded scientific analysis. But there is one piece of conventional wisdom that I have found to apply to the very biggest stream trout. They prefer inaccessible water which at the same time provides a good supply of food. Whatever cruised quietly in the eddy at the base of the cliff had both, and had them better than any other place in the last two kilometres of river.

In keeping with so many theories about trout and fly fishing, this wisdom falls short of being a rule. Once or twice I have waded up to my chest in freezing water, or risked my neck clambering down a steep bank. With dry mouth I have watched as the 'monster' sucks down my fly, only to find upon lifting the rod that it is transformed immediately into a prancing half-pounder. If you've done all this while angling alone, you can laugh

opposite: Mark Weigall casting to sippers on a quiet stretch of the Mitta River.

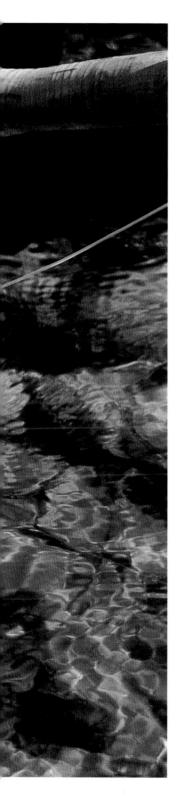

it off and keep fishing as if nothing has happened. However, if you have companions, and they have been summoned to watch while you defy the odds to hook the king of the river, expect a few unkind comments for the rest of the day, especially when a sprat rises: 'Look Phil, another whopper!'

I began to wade into the river, confident but not certain that I was about to fish for an exceptional trout. If I had to nominate a weight for 'exceptional' I'd say maybe two kilos, not an enormous trout for some waters, but here on the upper Swampy worth a special phone call to each of one's closest fishing friends. I couldn't see enough of the trout in the lee of the boulder to make any firm judgements about their size, but my hunch was that at least one would be of phone-call dimensions.

The flow on my side was stronger than it looked, and my feet struggled to find purchase among the greasy, football-sized rubble. I regretted that morning's choice of thigh waders instead of felt-soled wading boots. A third of the way across the river, water lapped at the lip of the waders and I could go no further. The soundless circles of the backwater trout were now within easy casting range, but three rod lengths of substantial current still lay between me and the nominal reverse flows behind the giant rock. If I landed my fly

left: A better-than-average rainbow from the upper Swampy, just below Geehi junction. Once, rainbows twice this size were common in both rivers.

above: Prime ant water awaits Peter when he finishes fishing this upper Murray riffle.

perfectly in front of a trout, it would only drift naturally for a second or two before line drag ripped it away. This risked spooking the fish.

Once more I considered the terrain of the far bank, the only place from which a drag free presentation could be made. Up close, it looked even more hopeless than I had originally thought. The cliff actually seemed to lean over the river. There was absolutely no ledge or shallow shelf from which I could have considered casting. My present position in the river was the solitary option.

Unconcerned about my dilemma, the two trout kept rising. I had now tied a smaller Royal Wulff—size 18—to the two kilo tippet. Though suitably small, it was still well

above: One of Rick Keam's flying ant patterns.

below: A beautiful trout from Dee Lagoon nears the boat on a day when we actually managed to fool a couple.

hackled, contradicting the logical need for a low floating fly. But it was a pattern that succeeded at least sometimes with ant feeders, the two bumps of peacock herl being quite ant-like in shape, and a bigger version had caught trout as recently as an hour before. Faced with a potentially big event, a small voice kept insisting that I give it a try.

In another box were a group of far more sensible flies: flying ants in brown and black with perfect translucent wings. They were designs commissioned from professional fly-tiers Rick Keam and Murray Wilson, both of whom had fingers more nimble than mine and patience to match. In any other situation I would have used them without hesitation. But although these ant patterns were perfect in theory, they had not actually been tested in the field. I lacked the necessary conviction that they would succeed. I might have only one chance at these fish, and I had to use a fly of faith, not an experiment.

In the flat afternoon light, my fly line flickered forward and back. I let instinct rather than aim guide my cast, stopping abruptly near the end of the final forward motion of my arm. Care overcame eagerness, and the line and leader gently piled on the backwater as intended, the fly perhaps twenty centimetres ahead of the most recent rise. The piling line would give me an extra second before drag ruined the presentation. For a moment, the little Wulff floated unobtrusively among the circling leaves and half-drowned insects and a moment was all it took. As if a diver's thumb and forefinger had plucked the fly by the very hook point, it was gone. I held my breath and lifted the rod.

It took perhaps three heartbeats before I realised I had a good, though not spectacular, trout on the end. The silvery brown fought hard and deep, toward the end even jumping. But I was in a hurry, and in two minutes it was lying among the river rocks, its flicking tail spraying my face as I removed the hook. A kilo or so, and a very nice fish. But not *the* fish. While such a trout would normally be a cause for that celebratory seat, a nice stretch and maybe even a muesli bar, this was not the case today. The trout had barely shot from my hands before I was already wading back out into the river; searching, hoping for more dimples behind the boulder.

And yes, the other trout was still feeding: clearly only the one now, but continuing to sip away with confidence. Had I snatched its companion into the current before it could be disturbed, or was the fish so focussed that it failed to notice the frantic warning signals of a hooked trout? Whatever the explanation, it was still there and could still be caught. Once more the little Royal Wulff sailed into the backwater, this time alighting almost on top of the trout. The water shimmered slightly, but what was sipped was not the Wulff but a tiny grey shape beyond it. Drag took the fly in the next instant, but thankfully behind the trout. The rises were appearing in sequence in a lazy circle the size of a living room, and when they were moving toward me again, I re-presented the fly. This time, there was a rise a handspan before, then a handspan after it. The pattern was now clearly rejected.

The status of the trout grew, but my confidence slipped. The casts were good but the fly was clearly wrong, at least for this fish. I considered other ant alternatives like a long dark emerger or a black-bodied pattern with wings of 'cul de canard' (duck rump feather), both of which had occasionally worked on ant feeders. Then I considered my predicament. With each presentation ending in unnatural drag, I wouldn't have many more chances. Sooner or later, the trout would see this and vanish. It was increasingly beginning to seem as if it was time to try Rick's ant.

above: A typical stretch of the upper Swampy Plains river—extremely rugged country where bottomless pools often block upstream passage. You must either swim, or bush-bash up over the cliffs and back down to the river again.

right: Landing an ant feeder on the Kiewa River.

The river water was cool, but the afternoon had grown more oppressive, and sweat trickled onto the inside of my polaroids as I tied on the fly, keeping one eye on the knot and the other trained behind the boulder. I considered upgrading my tippet, but the little ant would lose some of its appeal on nylon that was too thick. Besides, a tippet change would take time and I was worried the rises might stop in the meantime—big trout don't rise forever. A final pull on the knot and I cast again. The fly landed further ahead of the trout than I wanted, maybe a metre. Fortunately I piled the line well, and the pull of the main current was taking extra moments to draw the zigzags out. Then I lost sight of the fly. In the instant I glanced away at the line, the drab ant merged into the flotsam of the eddy. The trout took something: was it my fly? Decide! The world of the river slowed as my arm came up and the remaining 'S' in the pile cast hissed straight. In my mind's eye I can still see the instant when the fly would either zoom back past my shoulder, or the line come up tight under a bowing rod.

The line was tight.

Battles with large trout are usually associated with awesome runs that leave the angler struggling to keep some line on the spool. The reality is often different, and so it was with this fish. For several minutes it held its position deep in the backwater, not allowing even a glimpse of its size. An observer might have thought I was hopelessly snagged, rod held high and line singing to where it angled down into the river some ten metres away. But a closer look would have revealed sickening jerks of the rod tip, mirrored by jagged slicing of the surface where the line entered.

The trout felt huge, and I was too excited and apprehensive all at once to formulate any sort of plan. All I wanted to do was keep the line taut while avoiding any extra punches that would break it. It would have been a tedious struggle to watch, except that any fly fisher would have fully appreciated the underlying tension. I just stood there, and the trout just swam there. But ultimately the stalemate had to break, and when it did I was completely unprepared.

Without the slightest warning, the line went suddenly slack as the fish shot straight at me. I stripped like mad, stumbling backward at the same time, trying to regain a tight link. Just as I did, my heel caught between two rocks and I fell backward. Self-preservation is a strong instinct, so I don't really know how I managed to topple over while holding my rod hand high and letting the reel run free. Maybe the instinct to land

THE RIVER BEHIND THE HILL

a special trout is stronger! Soaked from the chest down, I struggled to my feet. At last I saw my fish. It had taken off downstream during my fall, but it was now head-shaking on the shallow side of the river and I could see its dark form against the sandy tones of the rubble. I splashed to the bank and walked toward it, retrieving a little line with each step. For the first time the trout thrashed on the surface, a dangerous move if the fly was poorly embedded. But the fish was tired now, and it did not follow through with a leap or those terrible rolls that end many a fight with a big brown when success is so near. Then its great hooked jaw was above the water gasping, and I pulled the fish steadily over the final shallows to a puddle cut off from the main stream. Barely submerged among the rocks, it lay on its side, eye turned down as if looking in disbelief at Rick's tiny ant protruding from its upper lip.

The trout was easily the best I had seen from our infrequent trips to this river. From the rod butt to within index finger length of the butt guide of my rod, a solidly built male brown trout with a worn pectoral fin and an ancient cormorant scar the only flaws in its perfect form. I would guess its weight at over five pounds, and I would have given a lot right then to be sharing the moment with an angling friend. But my brother was kilometres downstream investigating an unknown stretch, and it was just me and the fish. It crossed my mind to kill the trout—I still have enough childish pride that I would have liked to have seen Mark's face when I nonchalantly produced it back at camp. The thought didn't linger for long. I rarely kill big trout these days, and in any case we had already put two of pan-size in the Esky that morning.

I worked the fly carefully from a jaw lined with finger-gashing teeth, and lifted the trout slowly over the smooth rocks to the shallows beyond. At first he turned on his side, but as I rocked his dark form, fins flared and the gills worked more quickly. The spotted skin slipped from my grasp and the ant feeder swam out into the river with slow determination until he was lost forever among the eddies. I stood up, stretched and gazed up the valley to the east. Thunderheads that had been hinted at when the ants first appeared were now cresting Kosciuszko and her sister peak Townsend like the foam of a cataclysmic wave. Though the rumble of thunder was still far off, my walk back down the awkward valley would take time. With thoughts of a two foot brown trout to keep me company, I headed back toward camp.

below: The level of addiction to fly fishing can be measured by the number of rods owned. The differing power or 'weight' of various rods makes some suitable for small streams; others for windswept lakes. This fact lends a splash of legitimacy to those fly fishers whose rod collection is worth more than their car!

Flying Ants

Ant falls on rivers and lakes occur as an accidental by-product of ant colony migration, usually just prior to the onset of humid, thundery weather. They can also take place during still, settled weather in late autumn—particularly in the alpine foothills.

Of course, outside of the major flying migrations, ants still have the misfortune to fall into trout water all the time. This trickle of ants can be enough to bring the odd fish up on a regular basis, but the action never compares with a full-blown migratory ant fall.

Percentage-wise, ant falls are a comparatively rare event. A regular angler might only experience a couple of falls each season, though autumn falls in the mountain country can be somewhat more frequent.

However rare they are, fly fishers dismiss flying ants at their peril—I know, because I did the same once! As one of the most powerful stimuli to induce trout to rise, an ant fall can be the highlight of a fly fisher's year...or lowlight if you aren't carrying a flying ant pattern.

Murray Wilson's flying ant is an excellent pattern. It sits low in the water like a real ant, yet can be relied on to float. It is also comparatively robust. Murray ties a split body of black super-fine dubbing, clipped hackle legs in the centre, an underwing of cul-de-canard, and an overwing of 'zing'. Size 14 to 18 should cover most situations.

CHAPTER THREE

Thunderstorm!

A full-blown thunderhead cloud can hold half a million tonnes of water, and tower sixteen kilometres. That is over six kilometres higher than the 'boundary' of normal weather and reaches well into the stratosphere. Inside the cloud, updrafts may reach 140 kilometres an hour, strong enough to suspend a hailstone as big as a cricket ball. It will discharge five-centimetre-wide lightning bolts that travel at 128,000 kilometres a second and burn hotter than the surface of the sun. The rumble we call thunder is the sonic boom as air around a lightning bolt expands faster than the speed of sound.

opposite: A thunderstorm building over the Dargal Mountains in the upper Murray valley.

Summers in the northeast Victorian mountain country feature plenty of thunderstorms. That might sound like a recipe for brimming rivers, but it is not. With otherwise hot dry weather, and the storms only dumping their loads in localised bursts, the streams can get a little low by mid January.

The exceptions are the 'tailwaters' downstream from large reservoirs, artificially regulated to flow powerfully in summer and hardly at all over winter. The Mitta River is one such water. Here the unusual circumstance of a gentle summer flow can actually enhance the fly fishing. Not too low of course, but something less than the massive green volume that typically snakes its way to Lake Hume during summer. The icy water is effectively an artificial creation in both temperature and volume, and comes courtesy of releases from deep within Lake Dartmouth. While the trout thrive in 12°C flows that frequently reach ten billion litres a day, I prefer to fish the Mitta River at a more modest level when the pools and runs are clearly defined and the river can be safely crossed, at least at the broadest, shallowest riffles.

below: A Mitta River rainbow —much larger than the average—taken on one of Rick Keam's hoppers. Browns outnumber rainbows on the Mitta, but the latter are there in significant numbers all the same.

To encounter such conditions in January is a definite bonus. When longtime fishing friend Lindsay Waters, Mark and I first glimpsed a lower-than-normal river as we drove

past Tallandoon, the usual pre-trip optimism that seems to infect the car, even on trips when things don't really look too promising, was boosted to new heights. We were going to clean up, no doubt about it.

And over the next few days, the fishing did indeed manage to meet our high hopes. Glorious, settled summer weather persisted. While the temperature always climbed above 30°C by early afternoon, the heat was insufficient to make much impression on the super-chilled river, and the water temperature never made it beyond the high teens.

above: A muggy summer afternoon on northeast Victorian streams like the Nariel Creek is more often than not followed by some thunder and lightning.

By the afternoon of the third day the pace of the fishing had become less frantic, as tends to happen when every member of the party has caught more trout than they can easily recount. We parked the car deep beneath the canopy of an old willow, and found the time to simply sit in the shade and watch the glide in front of us while we ate lunch.

Eventually, a particular trout that had been rising sporadically beside the sword grass just downstream did so once too often. Lindsay stuffed a little too much sandwich into his mouth, sputtered something like 'see you later' and grabbed his rod. Mark and I followed a few minutes later, by which time Lindsay had already managed to hook his target on a Red Spinner and was trying to persuade the brown, which looked to be over a kilo, to come ashore.

A short conversation consisting of crude sign language, one-handed in Lindsay's case, and words that only half carried above the noise of the river, established that we would fish up and Lindsay would head downstream.

It didn't take long to locate rising fish ourselves, in this case one—no, two—trout sipping quietly in the bubble line towards the tail of the first pool. These flat-water sippers had proved more difficult than fish feeding in the swifter flows, but the pressure was off and I was only too happy to have a go. Mark was eyeing the delightful riffle above, so we parted company. I tied on a Highland Emerger. Created by Tasmanian fly-tier Barry Lodge to represent a hatching mayfly dun, this pattern is also a great generalist in other circumstances, particularly where glassy water demands a subtle, low-floating pattern.

The tail was surprisingly deep, and the trout further toward the far bank than they seemed at first. With a willow-restricted back cast, it took several tries before I finally got a good drag-free drift over the first fish. The trout appeared to take the emerger with confidence, but the perfect drift had come at the cost of a deep bow in the line. By the time it came up tight I felt the barest resistance before the fly pulled and sailed limply back behind me into the trees.

above: Peter Julian cradles a fine Upper Coliban brown, taken just after a thunderstorm. Prior to the storm the lake had produced nothing. It seems that thunderstorms— particularly on lakes— reinvigorate the trout, perhaps by oxygenating the surface.

Once I was back in action, it wasn't surprising to see that there was only one trout left feeding in the bubble line. My problem was the contrary currents between the rises and my position, so as it was a hot day anyway I decided to remove my vest and wet–wade out far enough to reduce the current problem. Casting a dry fly while chest deep in the Mitta was a novel experience, but worthwhile; on my second delivery the emerger was again sucked under and this time I lifted into lunging weight.

The trout was strong in the chilly water, but it lacked a powerful current to assist it and the pool tail was broad and unobstructed. Only patience was required to eventually guide the fish into the shallows. The brown was a fine hen, maybe shy of three pounds, but still well worth the trouble. I have to say, though, that strictly speaking I didn't land it—as I was reaching down the leader to twist the hook out, the trout rolled once and

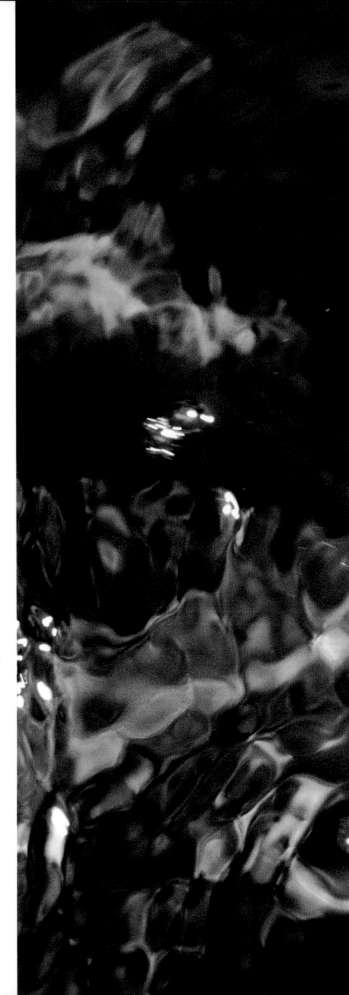

right: What we hope for on the Mitta (and don't always get)—a big-shouldered brown more than willing to take a Royal Wulff in broad daylight.

was gone! On a tough trip, or even a tough day, that would have been a significant disappointment. As an angler mainly practising catch and release fly fishing, I have a little rule that says I need to have the trout entirely in my control before I can honestly consider it to be caught.

In this case the fish followed dozens of recent captures, including a couple that were distinctly bigger. I instinctively waited for that slightly deflated feeling, but it didn't come. I headed off upstream to find Mark.

By this time, the tiny puffs of cloud that peeked over the ridges lining the valley had increased to airborne clumps of cotton wool, and I absently noted that perhaps a thunderstorm, common enough in northeast Victoria, was possible by evening. These events ruin the odd evening rise, but if they occur at the right time with the right intensity the fishing just before or just afterwards can actually improve.

It wasn't until I rounded two bends in the river that I found Mark, and it occurred to me that I had spent more time working on my sippers than I realised.

Sometimes you can tell how well a fishing partner has been doing without even having to ask. As I approached Mark, the way he was leaning forward with eyes glued to the progress of his Geehi Beetle suggested that he too had enjoyed plenty of action. Sure enough, when he caught sight of me he waded to the bank to report the capture of three fine trout, the largest of which had measured twenty inches against his rod butt.

By this time the clouds way over toward Mount Bogong suggested that a proper storm was already under way. The thunderheads were growing up and out like a slow-motion explosion of talcum powder. No such threat lay over the lower valley where blue sky still outnumbered clouds that were trying, but failing, to generate the strength for rain.

*above: Late evening success
for Peter during the calm
following a big storm.*

*opposite: Mark stalking trout
in the shallows, Mitta River.*

To our west the valley floor was quite narrow and ended in a steep forested ridge several hundred metres high. It was in that direction, away from the river, that Mark's eye first caught a peculiar sight. From behind this ridge a cloud formation had sprung up from nowhere, looking remarkably like a hand pointing toward the heavens. While the hand part seemed regular enough, the ever-thickening index finger that grew above it was unusual. I ventured that it could be the outer edge of a larger cloud mass hidden from view. Mark agreed that this was possible, so we decided to start fishing back downriver, nearer to the shelter of the car.

The growing cloud had come no closer by the time we reached the head of the pool in which I'd enjoyed the earlier action. With a clear view of the thunderhead hampered by the topography, we started to wonder if the bad weather was further away than it seemed. How often in the high country have you waited anxiously for a storm to hit, only to have it pass by kilometres away or fizzle out altogether before it arrives?

For all its stature, the apparently stationary cloud was beginning to look like a non-event, at least for this location. Our interest was easily distracted by the increasing number of rises appearing on the pool. When the sun broke through shortly after, Mark was busy casting to some nice slurps under the shade of a line of cottonwood trees, while I was giving serious thought to wet-wading toward a fish feeding close to the layered logs on the far side.

The valley was breathless and quiet under a veil of humidity accentuated by the burst of late afternoon sun. I decided that getting wet again to reach a fish was a pleasant option, and put a foot in the water. Right then I heard it: a strange roar coming from the direction of the ridge. A road hidden by trees cut across the lower third of the ridge, and my first thought was that a log truck or milk truck had lost control on one of the tight bends.

Mark heard it too, and simultaneously we turned to see not a truck flashing through the timber, but the whole forest on the upper ridge waving like long grass in a breeze. For a moment we were transfixed, unable to believe what we were seeing. Not a wisp of wind disturbed the area where we stood, but scarcely five hundred metres away the gums were thrashing like crazed voodoo dancers as the roaring sound raced down the hill in our direction. Towering above it all, the storm had somehow leapt suddenly over the ridge and was now looming troll-like over the main valley.

'Get back to the car!', I shouted, but Mark was already sprinting the hundred metres towards the Subaru hidden beneath two giant willows. I

suppose it took just a second or two from the time I first heard and saw the chaos on the hill to comprehend that a windstorm was about to strike, but it was nearly too long. Across the river flat, whole trees were torn up as the maelstrom bore down, headed by a vanguard of a million swirling leaves. I caught a glimpse of Lindsay, normally a cautious wader, prancing like a deer across the broad riffle just below the car. As I grasped the driver's door the full force of the storm hit. Two casts away a pump shed disintegrated, sending deadly sheets of corrugated iron racing through the air, the gusts tossing them as effortlessly as paper planes.

The overriding thought was to get the car and ourselves away from the willows. Thankfully Lindsay was jumping into the back seat as I drove flat out towards the open paddock. The rear view mirror revealed massive limbs falling in sequence where we had been standing only moments before.

The rain arrived shortly after in the company of relentless lightning and thunder, although the wind was fading as quickly as it arrived. The windstorm had lasted maybe

opposite: Gentle summer flow on the Mitta River.

below: Autumn glory on the Mitta River.

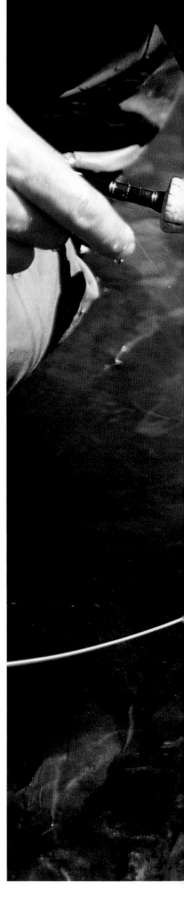

two minutes, but this was more than enough. Through swishing wipers the river was already revealed to be a dishevelled mess of branches, leaves and whole trees, as if in the aftermath of a huge flood. Iron and shedding lay randomly about us in the grass, and cattle stood stunned and motionless in small groups, still resolutely facing away from the now non-existent wind. The most sobering sight was the cottonwood grove from which Mark had dashed to the car. The fifteen-metre trees had been neatly trimmed of all branches on one side, while the top five metres had gone altogether.

No one in the car had much to say at first. We sat there with our own thoughts, trying to absorb where our sunny afternoon on a tranquil river had gone. Fifteen minutes earlier Mark and I had been discussing the best options for the evening rise. Now fishing of any kind seemed an impossible hope.

After a while Lindsay raised the question of what to do next. Look for a part of the river the storm had missed? Call it a day and head back to the caravan? Stay put, sit out the rain and hope that it cleared in time for a fish before dark?

Searching for a new, possibly unscathed area late in the day seemed a risky option, and in any case the thick cloud and veils of rain looked as if they filled the whole valley. Yet nobody was quite ready to cease fishing for the day, so we sat in the car and waited.

above: A thermometer is invaluable to fly fishers, enabling a quick and reliable assessment of stream temperatures. The Mitta and other tailwaters are largely immune from the warm summer water that can make trout in neighbouring streams inactive. I always take a reading though, just to be sure.

We watched expectantly as the rain slowly eased and the sky to the west began to lighten. Lindsay was already out of the car and assembling his rod as the last few drops hit the windscreen. But it was a cruel ruse. No sooner had the rain stopped than a fresh curtain came in from the north, and the downpour was as heavy as ever. Lindsay climbed back inside, obviously disgusted to see a potentially great evening lost. We all were, but with the unseen sun now gone behind the hills, there was nothing left but to return to camp and hope for a better day tomorrow.

As I drove out along the farm track it did occur to me that the loss of just one evening in a series of otherwise superb fishing days was hardly cause for complaint, but the faces of my companions suggested they weren't in the mood for 'chin up, chaps!' In any case, I felt fairly cheated myself.

We were a couple of kilometres along the bitumen when the rain suddenly stopped. Within seconds, the splash of water on the windscreen was replaced by the splat of insects. It was Mark who first noticed what they were—mayfly spinners in their thousands were being illuminated by the headlights as they tried to mate and lay eggs on

above: A mayfly spinner imitation. The colour is important by day, but in the fading twilight when the biggest falls occur on rivers like the Mitta, a dark fly can cast a silhouette more easily located by trout and angler alike.

the wet bitumen. Hundreds of metres from the river, the spinners had apparently been carried off course by the terrible winds of the earlier storm and now mistook the glistening road for their home water. With this bizarre spectacle came a troubling question: should we have stayed on the river after all?

We pulled over beside the main bridge before the campground and jumped from the car to check out the river. The light was almost gone from the western sky, but just enough remained to illuminate the centre of the long, straight stretch downstream. Drifting branches showed that this part of the valley had also felt the storm. Not so consoling were the rises. As far as we could see, the river was alive with trout feeding on a massive fall of spinners. This time it was Mark who raced for his rod, and even as he did the light fell another notch or two and the rises began to diminish. Was it worth the scrub-bash down to the river in the near dark with the rise failing and the light all but gone? Reluctantly we decided not.

Lindsay formulated a new motto that night—never give up on storm-lashed water. So far as I know, he's stuck to it ever since.

right: Flatter water—especially pool tails, then backwaters—is the best place to await the spinner feeders.

Evening Spinner Falls

On the mountain rivers of northeast Victoria and the Snowy Mountains a sprinkling of mayfly spinners can be found throughout the day, but evening is when the mating/egg-laying ritual really gets going. Throughout the warmer months, the soft sucking rises that dot the flatter water at last light are most probably caused by drifting spinners. During the hour or so before, mayfly duns or caddis may have been the catalyst for slashing, slurping rises—and some frantic sport! But look above the riffles and rapids after the sun disappears behind the ridge-tops, and there you will see the spinners dancing their last dance. At first they are too high above the water to attract anything but the leaping tiddlers. But about the time it starts to become difficult to tie on a fly without facing the western sky, the egg-laying females and dying males fall to the water.

Though trout take spinners in the fast, broken water, spinner feeders are best sought away from the turbulence, where their subtle riseforms can be detected in the half light. On nights when large duns, caddis or beetles have been plentiful earlier, a bulky evening dry like a Royal Wulff or Elk Hair Caddis may take them. Otherwise, a spinner imitation could be needed.

Don't be dismayed by the fact that these flies are nearly impossible to see in low light—with practice and confidence, you soon learn where your fly is to within a few centimetres...so that rise had to be to your fly. Strike!

After the rises have faded from most sections of the river, use that last smidgen of light to seek out the trout 'mopping up' in the side eddies and backwaters.

CHAPTER FOUR

The Eel Fisher

Autumn was fading. The days had become shorter than the nights, and the sun tracked far to the north. Even when it shone, its brittle light was not strong enough to heat the land.

Peter Murray and I arrived late in the afternoon at Lake Modewarre. Our destination was broad and oval shaped, quite featureless but for a large weedbed around the perimeter, marked by gaps and channels. Like many lakes in western Victoria, Modewarre is linked to a widespread but unspectacular volcanic past. The water lies in a shallow basin surrounded by small round hills and hardy yellow tussocks. Neither provided any

right: An old fenceline bears subtle testimony to the historic rise and fall in the level of Lake Modewarre.

shelter from the chilly breeze that came from the south, and the lake's steely surface was rippled with small waves that hissed on the sandy foreshore.

Despite our bleak surroundings, we felt the same excitement that arrival at a fishing destination always brings. The trout would not be bothered by the cold and wind, we theorised. In fact, these conditions were often more profitable on this water than balmy weather. So we donned beanies, woollen jumpers and parkas, and headed purposefully along the shore toward a promising channel.

Shortly after, Pete sighted a large trout crashing through the waves after galaxias on the outer edge of the channel. He waded quickly into the frigid water, and began casting his fly in the general direction of the disturbance. I wished him luck, and continued on my way, searching for a fish of my own.

below: A net is a handy accessory when landing large fish in weedy water. A good net should feature a soft, knotless mesh that will not harm the skin of the trout. Submerging the net so it is wet before use will also minimise damage to the trout.

Over the next hour I worked my way along the bank, casting here and there where the weedbed edge came in close, or around isolated clumps in the middle of the perimeter channel. I watched for signs of a feeding trout, and hoped for that sudden shock of life at the end of my

line. At length a single trout broke the water beyond the outer edge of the weedbed. Way past casting range, it offered the barest encouragement.

I had travelled another few hundred metres without event, when I sighted a distant figure moving slowly toward me from the opposite direction. Continuing along the lakeside, I could eventually make out a man carrying a couple of bulky objects. Then he stopped, and placed his bundles down beside him. I kept walking, half looking for trout in the waves, and half curious about the lone man ahead. The sun was now very low on the horizon, peering weakly through a veil of pink cloud. The wind had picked up, and it shrieked and moaned in the branches of a solitary dead tree. I looked back over my shoulder, and Pete was barely visible as a speck in the distance.

above: Peter Murray casting to smelters on a typically bleak late autumn day at Modewarre.

above: A typical brown trout from the Western District's Deep Lake.

I was now quite close to the mysterious stranger. Although the fading light robbed me of sharp vision, I could tell he was an old man. He walked with a pronounced stoop, and every movement was slow and deliberate. He glanced toward me, and I waved in acknowledgment. The old man nodded, and continued to labour with his assortment of bits and pieces, which as I approached were revealed as three bamboo fishing poles, a deck chair, a chipped esky and a rusty keeper net. I said hello, and asked him what he was fishing for. It was obviously not trout. 'I fish the eels,' he replied, in a heavy accent that I could not immediately identify.

Up close, he looked indeed an ancient man—how old I could not guess. His hands were as gnarled and coarse as the ancient hemp rope tied to his net. His face was deeply creased, and although the lines of age suggested a slight smile, his eyes were sad. He wore a patched blue greatcoat, and a thick black scarf. We chatted in the short and broken manner of two people who do not fully understand each other, but are happy to try. He seemed bemused by my fancy slim fly rod. 'For the trout,' I explained. 'Yes, the spotted fish,' he agreed. All the while he painstakingly rigged his poles with bait, and cast out his lines one by one. 'You Australia,' he stated. I smiled and nodded. 'I here fifty years from Poland. Not know if I Australia or Poland!' he exclaimed, and gave a short chuckle. I wasn't quite sure what to say to this, so I just chuckled as well.

By now it was nearly dark, and in spite of my heavy clothes, the cold had begun to seep through to my skin. The old man muttered something I couldn't catch, and bent down to light a battered kerosene lamp beside his chair. The soft glow of the light reminded me that it was getting late, and Pete was probably wondering where I was. 'I must go now,' I said. 'I hope you catch many eels.' The old man smiled and waved his hand, then looked back to his rods. I walked off into the night. The last I saw of him was a motionless silhouette in the lamp light, staring out into the black expanse of the lake.

above: Fly fishing vests are a blessing and a curse. They provide the owner with something of a portable storage system to carry the various odds and ends fly fishing requires. At the same time, all those pockets provide a temptation to haul around stuff that probably isn't essential. Some days I could swear someone snuck into camp at midnight and filled mine with bricks.

left: Pete and I walking back along the shore in full battle dress. Looking slightly ridiculous is the price you pay for staying warm and dry at a place like Modewarre in winter.

above: *Damselfly nymphs are an excellent choice at Modewarre and similar lakes.*

On the long walk back to the car, my thoughts weaved around the eel fisher. I calculated that he had left Poland around the end of the Second World War. Poland had been at the vortex of all the horrors that befell the world at that time. What had those sad eyes seen? Why and how did he leave his country? Who had he lost, or left behind? What memories played over and over in the mind of the old man as he gazed out into the night? I felt a surge of compassion for a man who seemed so alone, yet could still find a smile for a complete stranger.

A little later I approached the car, and Peter's shouted greeting brought me back to the present. 'How'd you go?' he asked. 'Pretty quiet—saw one move,' I replied, 'that's all. What about you?' 'Have a look at this!' he responded proudly, and drew a trout about two feet long out of a hessian sack in the boot. We both laughed out loud at his success, and I slapped him on the back and called him a fluky bastard, although I was just as delighted that we had a good fish to show for our efforts.

We threw off our jackets, placed our gear in the boot, and virtually jumped into the dry comfort of the car, shutting out the knife-edged wind with the clunk of the doors. Pete started the engine, but before he turned on the headlights, my eyes swept down the lake shore one last time. In all the cold blackness of the night, a single tiny light glowed in the distance.

right: *When you finally land one, a Western district rainbow makes all the work worthwhile.*

Modewarre and Other Western Victorian Lakes

Seasonally, the best time of year is spring. Summer is the quietest as surface water temperatures become excessive. As the temperatures begin to fall again in autumn, fly fishing improves once more. Winter is a mixed bag, providing bursts of very good fishing, but equally, many cold, grey and lifeless days.

Common Galaxias (*Galaxias maculatus*) and to a lesser extent, Australian Smelt (*Retropinna semoni*) are major prey for the trout of the Modewarre and the other western Victorian lakes. The Tom Jones, Hamills Killer, and the older Green Matuka are widely available and successful flies.

Rough, overcast days are likely to find the trout close to shore and in a feeding mood. On bright days, fish the windward shore or stick to dawn and dusk. Night fishing on all the lakes is definitely worthwhile outside of the dead of winter.

Polaroiding the calm water is possible at Lake Purrumbete, but the trout are extremely skittish. Speaking of wind, note that several lakes (especially Deep Lake and Murdeduke) can discolour severely in strong winds and may take a few days to settle.

CHAPTER FIVE

In the Wild

If you fish seriously for trout, you will spend some time in wild country after the sun has gone down. The evening rise ensures that at the very least you are bound to walk back to the car or tent in the dark. For some like me, the evening rise is often followed by a good hour or two of true night fishing, casting Black Muddler Minnows, Sunset Flies or other usually large patterns on a quiet pool or flat bay.

Evidently humans have an instinctive fear of the dark. As a species, we no doubt 'remember' the time, long gone for the most part, when our blunted sense of hearing, smell and sight made us

above: One of the best dry flies on mountain forest streams is the Geehi Beetle.

extremely vulnerable to the likes of leopards and wolves once night fell. On a rational level, an Australian night fisher has little to worry about beyond a sprained ankle or walking into a barbed-wire fence. We frequent areas that have long been devoid of any sizeable predator. For me, fear of the dark has faded with repetition. Countless hours roaming through the pitch black without incident has dimmed the nameless threats that dwell in my subconscious. Occasionally though, something happens to bring the fear of night crashing back to the fore.

As a teenager, I spent many days tramping through the wild and beautiful forests of the Otway Ranges. Mostly these trips had the ultimate objective of trout, but I'm glad to say that the pursuit was not so single minded that I failed to appreciate the journey as much as the destination. One such expedition brought my friend David and me deep into an Otway gorge to camp for a night. We had explored the place before, but the two-hour hike on top of a torturous car trip proved too much for a single day. An overnight stay would provide time to really enjoy the hidden valley and the fishing it offered.

We parked my ancient station wagon at the point where an old logging track had collapsed in a landslip long ago. Unpassable beyond, the track was rapidly being swallowed by the forest. For perhaps a kilometre its remains provided a route down into the valley that was marginally better than the surrounding jungle. Eventually, though, the fallen logs pushed us away from the track and down the steep mountainside. After much sliding and bush-bashing, and one or two cliff-top dead ends, we reached the river. Actually it was more of a creek than the so-called river denoted on the map. It was idyllic nevertheless, our first view revealing a gentle flow between mossy rocks forming a succession of pools and gurgling runs. At least a dozen different rising trout could be counted as far as the point where the stream disappeared behind an upstream bend.

Though the valley sides were steep enough to form frequent sandstone precipices, the floor was flat and up to a hundred metres wide. Giant mountain ash and blue gums were interspersed with beech, and their shade limited the understorey to treeferns, providing easy passage. The cool damp air that shrouded our little stream was from a different world than the dry summer heat that we had left behind in Melbourne.

David and I had intended to set up camp, and then fish. But with hours to sunset and the lure of rising trout, our rods were assembled at once. I doubt that anyone else ever went to the trouble of entering the upper valley as we had done. Though the trout were

opposite: Lindsay negotiating some overgrown water on the western slopes of the Otways.

abundant, they were small. In any event an inspection of the creek at the only road crossing well upstream would have revealed no trout to any would-be angler. Three or four kilometres below, the upstream passage of trout was blocked by two waterfalls.

Brightly coloured browns slashed eagerly at our Red Tags, and the weight of our packs was forgotten as we eagerly bypassed one another through the treeferns. Each leapfrog held the promise of some extra large pool where in turn a larger trout might dwell. In truth the few big pools yielded fish only marginally better than the standard ten to twelve inches, but the expectation was always there.

Long before true sunset, the sun's rays left the stream, and shadow began climbing the valley walls. Our desire for fishing temporarily sated, we sought a good campsite for the night. Before long we found a clearing, no larger than an average living room, covered in nothing but short green grass which the wallabies obviously grazed frequently. We wondered why this patch had not been overtaken by other plants. Perhaps in winter it was too sodden for larger vegetation to establish itself.

The tent was quickly erected, and with a stone fireplace created from the nearby river rocks and firewood gathered, the ideal campsite was set. A short walk upriver in search of an evening rise followed. While no real rise eventuated, enough trout took our flies in the blue-grey twilight to make the stroll worthwhile.

In the five minutes it took to return to the camp, night had swallowed the river flat. Soon the flicker of the campfire on the surrounding trees was the limit of our vision. From out in the dark came the calls of roosting birds, and the odd rustle or cracking branch as possums explored the trees. Except for campfire talk and the background murmur of the stream, the valley was silent.

Dinner was finished and the lengthy pauses in conversation suggested bed was not far away, when I saw a light through the trees. At first I was certain that my eyes were deceiving me, or that the firelight was reflecting off dew well away from the camp. But the night was dry, and even when I closed my eyes and looked again, the light was there. In a quiet, tense voice, I pointed out the light to David. He saw it at once, and the mood of sleepy relaxation around the fire was gone.

Although we tried desperately we could think of no reasonable explanation for the glow through the trees on the other side of the river. It was coming from the same level as us, and we knew the valley climbed steeply only eighty metres or so in that direction.

above: Stick caddis form a significant part of the diet of trout in many mountain rivers. While imitations are not the most glamorous of flies to look at, they can be very effective.

left: Alone on the Kiewa.

It could not be explained away as some distant source appearing closer than it really was—it had to be coming from right on the flat. We briefly toyed with the idea that other campers had somehow arrived in the very same part of the valley as ourselves, but the total lack of any other sights or sounds before or after dark made this theory implausible.

Under the benign light of a summer sun an unusual discovery on the river flat would have been cause for no more than curious exploration; in a lonely campsite surrounded by the black of night the inexplicable light became a sinister threat. Eventually the fear of not knowing outweighed the increasingly feeble security of the campfire. Whatever was out there, it could see us as well if not better than we could see it. I grabbed the tomahawk and trying to sound brave, told David I was going to investigate.

I carried a torch which I did not illuminate, preferring to find my way without alerting 'it' to my presence. There was just enough starlight to allow slow progress once my eyes adjusted to the gloom. Even so, I nearly slipped crossing the river, and unseen branches clawed at my face. Once on the other side, the forest understorey was so dark that I virtually had to feel my way forward. Meanwhile the strange light grew brighter as I approached. I could make out no silhouetted shapes, and during frequent pauses I could hear no sound. Oddly, as I felt my way toward it, the light became more distinct but did not appear to be getting any closer.

A glance over my shoulder showed that I had left our campfire well behind, and I knew that I must have almost reached the end of the flat. Strangely, though, the light still seemed some distance away. Feeling my way ahead, my hand suddenly found cold rock. Incredulous, I realised that I had reached the base of the cliff that bounded the flat, but the light seemed to be coming from within it…At once it all came together. As I ran my hand over the rock I found I was blotting out some of the light. The glow was coming from hundreds of tiny but amazingly bright points lining the cliff. I was able to scrape one off and it illuminated my whole palm. Glow-worms! I had heard of these creatures, but had no idea they could be found in Australia, let alone the Otways.

below: Wilderness trout are often modest in size, though numbers usually make up for it.

I turned on my torch and headed back to the camp, feeling at once relieved and foolish. The night had rapidly lost its threat and I even began to think about whether there was a nearby pool big enough to cast a Muddler and burn off some nervous energy.

Most frightening experiences around rivers at night can be explained by an unusual set of circumstances and over-active imaginations. I can recall another occasion in a cabin on the Howqua River when I awoke to the horrifying sight of a figure at my window, glowing red and swaying in ghostly rhythm. It took a few breathless moments to realise that the breeze had sprung up outside, fanning the coals of our supposedly extinguished campfire which backlit the fluttering curtains that in turn formed a vaguely human shape! Yes, most unnerving episodes can be similarly explained and laughed about, albeit a touch sheepishly, later on. But there has been one exception.

For many kilometres, the Thomson River has gouged an impressive chasm to the east of the Baw Baw plateau. It's not exactly a gorge, but it is several hundred metres deep and very wild, and until quite recently only a couple of rough jeep tracks dared to penetrate even a short distance into this patch of wilderness.

above: Seriously wild country—Franklin River headwaters, Tasmania.

above: An isolated stretch of the upper Mitta River.

Far above the river on the western side, the Thomson Dam road cuts a lonely swathe across the side of Mount Erica. This winding strip of bitumen is as close as most people get to the river which lies shrouded in tall forest and frequent mists way down below. I have fished the Thomson since before the dam was built. David Julian and I had an especially memorable trip many years ago into a section of the river that now lies under sixty metres of water. That little expedition was notable partly because we caught lots of trout, but mostly due to the fact that as crazy eighteen-year-olds, we decided we could survive three days on breakfast cereal, UHT milk and trout. Thank goodness we caught some trout. Even so, I can't look at Nutri-Grain today without having a momentary flashback to tepid milk and flies circling dirty enamel bowls.

These days, the Thomson doesn't seem to be the great fishery it once was, and in any case my favourite stretches are submerged beneath thousands of tons of water. But before the dam was completed, even the section in the gorge below it was first class trout water. It was back then that I planned a day's fishing in its most remote section. The idea was for my friend Ian to drop me by the side of the road at the top of one of the overgrown tracks leading to the river. He had no time available for fishing that day, and had kindly offered to pick me up in the evening somewhere on the road further up the valley. Thus I would be able to walk down to the river and fish upstream for several hours. One evening, I planned to cut up the mountainside at a favourable spur line knowing that I would hit the road after a steep climb through the forest.

With mist still hanging in the hollows, Ian stopped the car at the point where an old jeep track plunged perilously away from the road down a ridge toward the river. I grabbed my rod and day-pack out of the boot. 'See you somewhere on the road about eight,' I said. 'Catch one for me!' yelled Ian as he U-turned back toward

above: The Black Muddler works well on wild country trout at night—if you're game to head out after dark in the first place!

town. The car disappeared around a bend in the forest, and the valley turned silent once more. I threw the pack over my shoulder and headed off down the steep eroded track toward the river, delighted to be exploring new water.

The day promised to be pleasantly warm, if overcast. High cloud hinted at rain in a day or two without being threatening: good fishing weather. A twenty-minute scramble down the mountainside brought me to the water's edge. I tried not to think about the walk out at the other end, which would probably take the best part of a steep uphill hour.

The currents hissed and rumbled, but the river could be crossed with care in a few places where the gravel beds were wide and the flow spread out. Within ten minutes of arrival I had a half-kilo brown trout that happily scoffed a Grey Wulff drifted along the bank. The fishing over the next few hours was of the kind we rely on to keep us going through the tough patches. I wondered briefly if anyone else had cast a line on this stretch of water in the last year, or even the last decade. Realistically, it was almost certain that others fished this difficult-to-reach piece of the Thomson. But not a single boot print could be seen in the soft sand, not a solitary snack bar wrapper, and I could at least toss the idea around without proof to the contrary.

right: Wild water and a wild Thomson trout.

The hours slipped away as they do when the weather is good and the fishing better. By mid-afternoon I decided a break was called for, and a waterworn boulder beckoned as a natural easy-chair. I sipped some water from the river, then sat back on the 'seat' and munched a sandwich. My eye lazily followed the sweep of the water, then soared up the near vertical cliff face opposite, until the rock blended with the forest higher still. My gaze drifted back to the polished rocks on the sandbar before me, when a strange shape in the sand a few metres distant caught my eye. I wandered over to have a closer look.

There was no mistaking the shape—I was looking at the largest paw print I had ever seen. Almost certainly it belonged to a dog, though it was nearly as big as my hand. It looked old and I could find no other prints nearby, but I cast a wary glance around me all the same. Nothing moved in the silent forest or around the murmuring river. I shook off all thoughts of giant dogs and resumed fishing.

A couple of hours and several trout later, the weak sunshine left the valley floor. In the gathering gloom I began to look for a crossing back to the western bank from where I could

above: Putting the bull theory to the test on the Jamieson River. The only way to reach a trout rising just downstream was to pass this ton or so of Angus. The fact that I'm still here to write this suggests my Uncle's advice was correct—at least this time!

make the long climb up the ridge to meet the road and Ian's lift. I'd kept a couple of fat trout for dinner, and though I knew the walk uphill through the thick undergrowth would be tough, there was no question in my mind that the fishing had been worth it. Then in the midst of happy thoughts of fried trout and cold beer, the chilling sensation of being watched cut through me.

I swept the surrounding river banks for signs of life, but except for the odd trout swirling in the current, there was not a living thing to be seen. The thick bush on the steep slopes above was silent and still. With mock bravado, I began casting my fly once again as if all was normal, but the feeling only grew stronger. I absently followed the course of the little fly as it bobbed past me a dozen times, and then suddenly there it was. As if from nowhere, an enormous dog had abruptly appeared and stood motionless in the middle of the gravel bar on the far bank.

My first impression stays with me to this day: one of tiny, cold eyes gazing at me from a wolf-like head that seemed far too big for such pinpricks of light. A faded dingo tan in colour, the dog had a shape like an Alsatian, only taller and heavier. The ears were dingo-like, but again they were too small. Overall, in size and appearance the animal appeared quite abnormal, indeed almost a freak.

Initially my pulse raced and my instincts screamed at me to flee, but with effort I pushed such thoughts away and concentrated on maintaining a calm facade. I recalled my uncle's advice as a child when crossing a paddock shared with a huge black bull: 'Show no fear—animals can sense fear'.

Slowly my breathing subsided and I took stock of the situation. The dog faced me on the other side of a deep pool, and it would have to swim the cold current to reach my bank. Also, its attitude appeared neutral: neither aggressive nor afraid, though I imagined I sensed malice in its stare. With feigned casualness I searched for a stout piece of driftwood, just in case. Then I turned my back on the dog and sauntered off upstream. Every so often, I glanced back to find the animal keeping pace on the western bank. Time had passed quickly, and before I knew it the light was fading fast in the valley.

below: Remote water on the Indi River near Murray Gates, Kosciuszko National Park.

I looked at my watch—a quarter to eight! Ian was meeting me on the road in fifteen minutes. I considered my options. I could stay on my side of the river, but I remembered the paw print, and knew that the dog could cross the river eventually if it chose. The thought of coping with that situation in the dark held little appeal. My only way out was up the slope on the dog's side of the river. The decision was made. I would cross the river and attempt to climb the slope while it was still light. If I had to face the dog, I would at least have my eyesight, for maybe twenty minutes anyway.

Without further debate I walked briskly up-river to a likely crossing point. I glanced back downstream, expecting to see my adversary. But in the space of seconds, the dog had vanished. In one sense, this bothered me even more than being able to watch it across the river. Better the enemy you can see…However, every passing minute robbed me of precious light, so I waded into the river and forged across the thigh deep current. My wrist ached from my grip on the stick as I reached the dog's shore, but there was no sign of it. I made one last scan of the surrounding undergrowth and river bank, then plunged up the forested mountainside.

At first I walked quickly up the steep slope, pushing aside tree-ferns, stepping over fallen logs, warily avoiding loose rocks. Then I began to jog. It was a mistake in such precipitous terrain, but I was tired, nervous and worried that I'd miss the rendezvous. I broke through branches, stumbled and fell on invisible obstacles, then ran again. Suddenly, against the noise of my breathing and breaking sticks, I heard another: the sound of something else crashing through the forest behind me. Gasping for breath and terrified, I nevertheless turned to face my pursuer, my heavy stick providing scant comfort. Almost at once a dark shape burst into view metres away…then shot past me. Only a wallaby! But the millisecond of relief evaporated as I caught a snapshot of its eyes, wide with terror and oblivious to me.

The crashing of the wallaby died away, and I stood poised in the black forest with the blood pounding in my ears, the stick gripped with both hands. Silence. I strained to hear something, anything. Even the river could be heard murmuring far below, but nothing else, not a sound. Then right at the very edge of my perceptions, I thought I heard a soft grunt to my left. I strained an ear in that direction, and searched the dark scrub for any trace of movement. Nothing.

I don't know how long I stood on that spot, but slowly I began walking again, half forwards, half backwards, every nerve alert for attack. Higher and higher up the mountainside I climbed, but aside from the distant crack of a single twig, I saw and heard nothing more. Finally a dim light appeared through the trees ahead of me, and in a few more steps I broke out of the forest's clutches onto the starlit road. Only a few metres wide, it felt like a football field: an oasis of air and space and soft light. I sat in the middle of the road, still clutching my stick, and waited for Ian. I was half an hour late for our rendezvous.

Ten minutes later I heard a car approaching, and shortly headlights could be seen sweeping the forest ahead. The vehicle rounded the bend in front of me and I frantically waved it down. The driver pulled over and turned off the engine—to my relief it was indeed Ian. 'Where've you been?' he almost shouted. 'This was my last look for you, and then I was going back to raise the alarm!' He paused, and then dropped his voice. 'What happened to your face?' I rubbed my cheek and could feel the warm trickle of blood where a branch must have gouged me in the dark. Exhausted, relieved and cold all at the same time, I didn't know where to start.

right: Geehi valley, over-shadowed by 2,200 metre Mt Townsend and the Main Range is considered to be some of the mainland's most rugged trout country.

Forest Streams of the Otway Ranges and Southern Victoria

These streams are best fished from November through to the end of April. Outside of these times the valleys become increasingly cold, clammy and lifeless, and trout activity plummets accordingly. Frequent early season spates bring flows that are too high and discoloured for truly enjoyable fly fishing.

Once air temperatures warm up and flows settle down, the tree and shrub cover overhanging the streams ensures that beetles and other terrestrial insects become important to the trout. Flying ants are also a possibility on humid days. The generally protected catchments encourage high water quality which in turn favours mayflies. Fly fishers should watch out for spinners and duns from late afternoon onwards.

Royal Wulffs and Red Tags are consistent producers. The trout rise well and, outside of heavy hatches, are usually opportunistic rather than selective feeders. On those occasions when the trout won't come to the surface, try a scruffy brown nymph with a black wingcase, ribbed with copper wire.

Whatever the fly, pay special attention to the heads of the pools and the faster water between, especially the riffles. Don't be put off by lack of depth.

CHAPTER SIX

The Fishing Report

He wore a black hat and was obviously new to the fly fishing game. His back-cast was slowly trimming the weeds along the shore of Upper Coliban Reservoir. That his fly line continued to remain airborne seemed a miracle of physics. I was grateful for the considerable distance that separated his fishing position from mine. In fact, in addition to whipping the water before him with a ferocity that would make a bullock driver blush, Black Hat did not seem content unless his wading produced a bow-wave large enough to travel to the other side of the bay. From my crouched position among the bushes, I hoped

right: Matt Stafford and Lindsay swapping yarns on Cairn Curran while they wait for the sun to dip a bit lower.

opposite: On the Thredbo River—will there be a story to tell by day's end.

above: The honesty stick!

fervently that I remained inconspicuous casting to the occasional swirls of trout about ten metres offshore. I wasn't exactly sure what these fish were feeding on. Emerging midges or maybe drifting snails? Nothing could be seen on the surface. I changed to a small black nymph. Another trout barely betrayed its presence in the light ripple to my right, then swirled again slightly closer. Judging its speed and direction as best I could, I cast the nymph, let it settle briefly, then began a slow retrieve. After a few twists of line, a firm pull was matched by a sub-surface boil, and a silvery brown immediately slashed the surface. The 900 gram fish was surprisingly difficult to subdue, and to my intense dismay I realised its antics had caught the attention of Black Hat, who was now reeling in and simultaneously crashing through the shallows like a wounded hippo toward my little corner of the bay.

I beached the fish and was twisting the hook out to release it when my nemesis arrived, his progress foreshadowed by a shower of spray. 'GOT ONE, DID YOU?' he bellowed so loudly that I instinctively searched the far side of the lake for the invisible companion he must have been addressing. Finding no sign of anyone else, I had to draw the puzzling conclusion that his shout was directed at me.

'Yes, got this brownie,' I replied. 'Had to keep low and out of the water though—they're very easy to spook this morning'. He nodded in whole-hearted agreement, while absently flicking a clump of weed off his wader with a force that would have kicked a goal from sixty metres.

'SPOOKY ALRIGHT!' he said, waving his white-sleeved arms around him for emphasis, as if directing an F-18 landing on an aircraft carrier. I nodded in resignation as the last swirl nearby turned into a departing bow-wave.

Unperturbed by my indifference, Black Hat launched into a new subject. 'Yeah, down at Bullen Merri yesterday … got a four pounder! … and a six pounder…' He paused. I could see his mind ticking over. Bullen Merri was a fabulously rich water, and had historically produced many 'double figure' fish. Could he get away with an even more outrageous claim? Yes! '…And a twelve pounder!' he exhaled, almost in a sigh of relief that he had managed to squeeze out the final huge 'porky'.

I did my best to contain a smirk as I formed a mental picture of this previously unknown strain of Bullen Merri rainbows that were suckers for the sound of fly line whipping the water. But the entertainment value of Black Hat's antics was fast wearing out, so I excused myself and walked off down the shore, leaving him vigorously oxygenating the water in the precise place where I had caught my fish. No doubt he couldn't believe his luck at securing the hotspot!

There would be few fly fishers, myself included, who would fail to register a bleep or two on the lie-detector when asked if they had never exaggerated or extended the

below: The foundation of a long story!

truth during their fly fishing career. It's easy to 'round-up' the weight of a released fish. After all, it can be hard to estimate such things, especially in poor light! And 'caught about half a dozen' has a better ring to it than 'five', while 'yeah, got a few' sounds more impressive than 'caught two'. Mostly, modest extensions on reality are pulled off rather nicely, because other fly fishers enjoy the encouragement that is offered by another's success, and are only too happy to grant benefit of the doubt so long as the claims fall within the realms of credibility.

Where the likes of Black Hat come undone is when their enthusiasm to impress others runs away, to the extent that they end up so far outside the boundaries of possibility that not even the most generous of listeners can believe them. If Black Hat had stopped at one four pounder from Bullen Merri, okay. I mean, even novices get the occasional lucky break. But when he added a six pounder his credibility was evaporating quickly. And of course the claim that transported him into the arena of outright fibber was the twelve pounder. Hopefully with practice, Black Hat may learn the subtleties of telling fishing tales to the point where he keeps his audience interested.

Fishing stories are the next best thing to actually fishing. When my friends return from a trip away, I look forward to their reports almost as much as a pending expedition of my own. They all know the art of delivering a good report. The phone rings: 'Hi Phil, it's Pete—I'm back.' 'Pete! How did you go'? (no mucking around with small talk).

At this point, Peter knows not to say 'got a six pounder in Great Lake'. Rather, he starts at the beginning: the plane trip over, snow on the Western Tiers as he drove through the dark, cat-ice in the shallows the following dawn, the first five tailers refusing the fly,

above: 'Remember that big brown you got down at the poplars last year, Pete?' Building the anticipation on a Jamieson River evening.

above: Mudeye patterns, like this one by Rick Keam, account for many large trout every season.

above: Stalking a west coast estuary, hoping for a sea trout worthy of a report.

and so on. By the time the story arrives at the point where the six pounder does grab the fly, the experience isn't too different to having been there yourself to see it.

There is only one rule regarding fishing stories in our group: no calls from the field. A 'call from the field' is one made either from a mobile phone whilst the caller is actually fishing, or from a phone box nearby, while the receiver is stuck at work. I once phoned Lindsay at his office from outside the Newlyn store to tell him I'd just caught a four and a five pounder. He hung up on me before I could tell him I was about to duck back and try for another.

Fishing stories have value in addition to pure entertainment. No source of information can match a fresh report from a fly fisher you know well. When you are familiar with the angler, you can fill in the blanks and get a fairly objective picture of what the fishing was really like. Or more accurately, how much you would have enjoyed it, and therefore how hard and how fast you should try to get to the same waters they've just fished.

My more exuberant friends give great reports, but it helps if you also know that they're always happy just to be out fishing. The trip has to be pretty awful before they'll concede as much. I think my own reports probably come out much the same. It is enough if some trout could be located, even if they couldn't be easily caught. Just one successful session in an otherwise lean few days is enough to rate a water or an area 'good'. We say things like: 'Well, there were plenty of fish to be polaroided. Another couple of days of warm weather and they would have been going for the dry.'

Conversely, quite a grim report from the conservative members of my fishing circle can still whet my appetite. The fact that 'really big trout were moving in close most evenings, but no one could catch them' doesn't exactly cause me to cross a potential destination off my list. Of course this means that I sometimes race off to a particular water with visions of cracking the code, only to find that the big trout referred to are indeed quite impossible to catch.

I guess the ideal fishing report lies somewhere between this last category and what Black Hat would say. It would be cold blooded about the essential facts, but overlaid with enough boyish enthusiasm to make you wish you had been there too.

The Coliban System, Central Victoria

Upper Coliban Reservoir, Lauriston Reservoir and Malmsbury Reservoir form a chain of water storages on the upper Coliban River, a little over one hour's drive north of Melbourne.

The central storage, Lauriston, is primarily steep-sided and has the most stable water level of the three. The northwestern sections sometimes provide good daytime dry fly fishing to beetle and grasshopper feeders during summer and early autumn, though really hot days should be avoided. Smelting also occurs, particularly during late autumn and early winter.

Upper Coliban is the largest storage and the most prone to fluctuating water levels. Extensive gently sloping shores exist in several bays, and when rising water covers these in spring, excellent wet fly fishing for floodwater feeders can result. Smelting trout are a possibility throughout the year, and midges feature in the cooler months, particularly if levels are high.

Malmsbury offers some floodwater feeders in the southern bays, but heavy fishing pressure confines activity to dawn and dusk outside of weekends. As with the other two lakes, smelting trout are a feature. In mid-spring on this lake and the others, dun hatches can occur. The intensity and duration of the emergence varies from year to year. In some springs there are too few duns to bother with, but every second or third year, enough hatch to bring up the trout.

CHAPTER SEVEN

Dawn

Some people are born carrying the 'early riser' gene. These types seem to know how lucky they are compared to the rest of us, and don't mind saying so. Especially on a fishing trip. Early risers come out with irritating comments like 'the half hour before sunrise is the best time of the day', 'rise and shine!' and 'my brain works like new first thing in the morning'. Stay away from them at breakfast, because they'll want to have an intelligent conversation.

The only good thing about early risers is that their boundless energy usually runs out sometime in the middle of the evening. Around eight, they

above: Rob Sloane's Fur Fly has become a standard for fishing flooded lake margins in Tasmania.

below: A dawn sky like this in the Tasmanian highlands carries the threat of bad weather before the day is out. 'Red sky at morning…'

settle into a deep chair pretending they're going to read a book or fill in an entry in their fishing diary. Five minutes later the rhythmic snoring begins. If they really got up your nose with their chirpy comments fourteen hours earlier, this is your cue to drop a frying pan or two on the stone floor of the cabin kitchen. Better yet, slap them on the shoulder, throw a vest in their lap, and announce in your heartiest voice 'Come on, time for some night fishing!'

If I seem a little resentful of early risers, it's probably because I wish I was more like them. Well, sometimes. Dawn is supposed to be a great time for catching trout, and as a committed fly fisher, it follows that I should spend a good deal more time on the water at this hour than I actually do.

For quite a few years, I persuaded myself and anybody who cared to listen that dawn wasn't as productive as people said. The fact is that I based this belief on too few dawn trips to really make any reasoned judgments. And I must admit that some ill-thought-out sorties stuck in my memory and cancelled out the more successful ones. Like the time Lindsay and I headed out to Newlyn Reservoir in the dark of a frosty winter's night (what were we thinking?) to be blasted off the water by a stinging cold front before the sun even came up. Sessions like that really put a dent in your early morning attitude, especially when the alternative had been a warm sleeping bag in front of the fire in Geoff's shearer's quarters.

I still argue, though feebly, that dusk is often better. But there are at least some places where it is simply sacrilege for a fly fisher to stay in bed when night is moving toward the new day. Tasmania and its highland lakes is one such place. In spite

of all my negative thoughts about getting up before the sun, I can't even hear the word 'Tassie' without experiencing a flood of images—dead calm lakes, misty first light, and big trout feeding in every likely spot with a strange mixture of subtlety and majesty.

When I first read Rob Sloane's *The Truth About Trout*, the section he included on tailers at dawn sounded just too perfect. Sure, if you could pick the right morning, no doubt you would sometimes encounter large trout finning slowly through ankle-deep shallows. Locals have the luxury of being able to choose the right moment to go out. As a visitor, it seemed too much to expect that we would be able to find the fishing that Rob so enticingly described.

But right from the first trip, the dawn tailers were there as promised. After a succession of journeys to Tasmania, we decided to bring a video camera to get some evidence for disbelieving family and friends. Of course the camera stayed safely in the car for the first couple of mornings, as nobody wanted footage so badly that they would

above: Trout rising in a Murray River backwater at sunrise. Fish like these have often disappeared back into the main flow by the time the sun hits the water.

sacrifice fishing for filming. Eventually, on the third morning, some Bronte Lagoon tailers were recorded. By that stage, we had caught a sufficient number of the very difficult trout to begin to think about actually capturing some of the action on film. I don't remember how it was that I ended up carrying the camera while Mark and Lindsay fished. I do remember deeply regretting it when we walked down to the lake and there were trout everywhere. I knew we had still five more dawns ahead of us, but that didn't count for much at the time. I saw big trout and I wanted to fish. You know how it is.

With considerable misgivings I stuck with the camera, leaving my fly rod against a tree well back from the lake. Lindsay went left, Mark to the right, and I panned between them. Urgent grunts or the frantic sound of stripping line were my cue to focus on one or the other. Through the little television of the viewfinder I was able to look at the scene as a true observer for the first time. Bronte at dawn was as beautiful and tranquil as the

above: Matt Stafford looking for inshore swirls on Upper Coliban at first light.

opposite: The early bird catches...the monster! Ray Matthews with his reward for setting the alarm.

left: Early morning mist on the Mitta.

right: Searching the margins of the Malmsbury Reservoir at daybreak.

world can ever be. At the same time a silent but powerful undercurrent of excitement rippled in the glimpses of fins and tails, and the tense poses and creased brows of my companions. When we play the tape now, you can hear me shouting questions to Mark and Lindsay: 'Did you cover that fish?' 'Did he take it?' 'Is that two different trout in front of you?' There is never a reply. They are so focussed that they simply don't hear me, or if they do, there's no room left in their concentration to deliver a reply.

As the light grew brighter, and the sun first struck the tree tops at the western edge of the bay, the trout slowly moved out and could be seen less and less. Dawn was slipping away. The realisation broke the spell and I changed from very amateur cameraman back to angler, and ran for my rod. One trout had continued to feed in a tiny pocket encircled by weed right in front of me throughout my stint with the camera, a titbit of information I had kept to myself.

opposite: Even after the first rays of sun arrive, the trout in Tasmania will often continue fossicking in the food-rich shallows for an hour or more. Lake St Clair.

Breathlessly I arrived back at the pocket. The weeds in one corner rippled slightly—it was still in there! I cast a floating green nymph to the edge of the weed. The tiniest of dimples and bulges in the surface film indicated the passage of the trout as he stalked over to my trap and gulped it down. I lifted with amazing control given the situation, and a

golden three pound brown went tearing out into the bay, leaving a web of startled bow-waves from several nearby trout in its wake. I landed that glorious trout, and it was worth ten of its brethren from any familiar water back home.

above: Fly reels are relatively simple, with no gearing and a basic knob handle. Most of the time they are little more than humble line storage devices—until a big trout strikes and you need the back up of a good drag system.

Sometimes when my fishing friends drop over, we play that video. It's wobbly in places, I panned too fast, and my breathing is sometimes picked up by the mike, like something from a B-grade horror movie. You almost expect Mark and Lindsay to be suddenly rushed by a poorly made-up monster.

For all its faults though, the audience is invariably captivated, except for any non-fishers who politely shuffle off and make a coffee or something after the first couple of minutes. The rest of us stare as if we were watching real tailers. There's often some commentary from the audience: 'Did you see that one in the bottom corner? Mark should have cast to that one.' And we all laugh at the bit where Lindsay gets his backcast caught in the pin-rushes (we're a heartless group!). When the film is over, those who haven't been to Tassie often start asking about how to plan a trip there. The rest of us are already doing just that.

right: A brand new day in the Indi Valley.

Tailers at Dawn

The extreme shallows of many Tasmanian lakes offer trout a feeding area that is not being continually cropped. Fear of exposure to predators keeps the fish offshore when the light is bright, allowing life in the margins to rest. Evidently, this creates a significant increase in available food compared to deeper shores. This is what brings the tailers in under the cover of grey choppy days, sunset, and—especially—dawn.

There are two broad categories of 'tailer', although there is some overlap. Dawn is the best time for both. The first kind are the trout feeding on slow moving aquatic life—snails, scud, stick caddis and small crustaceans. These are the fish for which the term 'tailer' was first coined—leisurely browsers, often feeding in the head down, tail up position so fascinating to anglers. Pin-point presentation of small, inert wet flies (like a Stick Caddis or Fiery Brown Beetle) is often necessary to even get a take, and then detecting the take itself is difficult.

The second kind of tailer is arguably better described as a shallow water forager, or floodwater feeder. Such trout are lured into newly inundated shallows to feed on flooded terrestrials like earwigs, worms, grubs and beetles, or frogs and tadpoles. They are inclined to move faster than true tailers, and act with a strange mix of aggression and nervousness. They also display less fin and tail. These trout are often more catchable than the first kind, and with an array of prey on their menu, can often be fooled by a range of flies, whether wet or dry, retrieved or stationary. Floating nymphs or Rob Sloane's Fur Fly are particularly effective.

Spring is the best time for tailers, though they are a possibility throughout the Tasmanian season. Tailers require practice to locate. Start by looking for *anything* unusual—a dimple, a moving pin-rush stem, a subtle swirl—not a whole back or tail.

CHAPTER EIGHT

Not According to Plan

The journey Lindsay and I made to Tasmania in September 1993 is memorable for being about the best I have experienced for tailers at Little Pine Lagoon. Even if you have never fished for them, you have probably heard about the remarkable and exasperating 'untouchables' that inhabit this small, windswept and otherwise unspectacular highland lake.

As the trip turned out, it is also memorable for other events of an entirely unscheduled nature. But first, to the fish.

I regard stalking tailers anywhere as just about the cream of fly fishing, although I concede that in many places the term itself is rather misleading. Trout foraging in water mere centimetres deep are incredibly adept at keeping out of sight. The devotee of tailers must generally learn to discern the merest dimple, the tiniest tip of fin protruding from the water as a clue to the whereabouts of the feeder.

This can be the case at Little Pine too, but just as often the tailers justify their name by waving a whole tail in the air, plain as day. This brazen behaviour can take some time to register on those of us used to more discreet signs. I remember staring straight through the first few tails I 'saw' at Little Pine, my brain apparently computing 'too obvious —can't be trout'. Once you realise that those great big flags really are the tails of brown trout head-down in the weed searching for delectables, it seems too good to be true.

above: Fresh snow dusts a tangled thicket in the Tasmanian highlands.

The venerable John Brookes, who at twice my age can place a fly with twice my accuracy, insists that these head down/tail up fish are the ones for which the term tailer was originally coined. He takes exception to the subsequent broadening of the definition to include any trout that happen to sneak around the shallows showing an occasional glimpse of fin. 'They're just shallow water foragers, Phil,' he says, 'not befitting of the term "tailers" at all!'

At any rate, there soon comes a sobering realisation that seeing them is one thing but catching them is another. Tailers foraging over newly flooded ground for terrestrial insects and frogs can be quite accommodating, but those grubbing for aquatic creatures like amphipods and snails are rarely obliging. Little Pine fish usually fall into the latter category.

right: Searching for tailers in the flooded margins of Bronte Lagoon.

above: The Fiery Brown Beetle is one of the first flies I'll try if I encounter tailing trout.

Successful Little Pine anglers have quite different methods of catching the tailers. Some fish with nothing but a small, nondescript dry like a Coch-y-bonddu. The trout are not rising, but they figure that sooner or later a perfect presentation will be enough to induce a fish to take off the top in such shallow water. Another bemusing tactic is to rip a big matuka or similar wet past the trout. You can watch an angler doing this and shake your head patronisingly as most fish flee in fright, but then inexplicably the odd fish will slash savagely at the supposedly inappropriate fly. Suddenly the poor fellow you were feeling sorry for a moment ago has a nice brown on the bank.

The 'proper' way to fish to Little Pine tailers is with a small, inert wet fly that bears at least some resemblance to the crustaceans and snails the fish are feeding on. This is fly fishing at its most exacting. First you need to locate a trout. Not so hard. As I have described, the true tailers are quite easy to find if they are working at all. The next problem is to actually track a trout you have found. This can be more difficult, because they don't leave their tails out all the time. If there is any wind (for which Little Pine is legendary) there will be ripple on the water, and the minuscule disturbances the tailers make between tail and fin displays are hard to detect. Yet detect you must, because it is essential to judge speed and distance to present the fly in exactly the right place. The trout must virtually crash into your fly for there to be any chance of a take. Nose down in the weed and preoccupied with the bugs in their immediate vicinity, they rarely deviate more than a finger's length to take the fly.

below: Waiting for the tiniest swirl, or the faintest twitch of the leader, Little Pine Lagoon.

So to the third difficulty—putting the fly in a target area no bigger than a saucer, and at precisely the right moment to attract the trout's interest.

The final hurdle is noticing the take. If you are lucky, your tippet will move the merest fraction. But often the trout are travelling so slowly that they can scoff your fly, chew it and spit it out without your leader reflecting a thing. It was Lindsay who persuaded me to adopt the 'if in doubt, strike' approach. If a trout swirls or boils right where your fly is, lift the rod regardless of whether the leader moves. Of course sometimes you strike into thin air and the trout bolts for cover, but just as often, a rewarding weight greets you.

Fishing to genuine Little Pine tailers is a game of percentages no matter which method you employ. Rarely can you expect a response from every trout covered; instead, you must rather present well to as many fish as possible and hope that at least a fraction of them will oblige you with a take.

above: Persistence pays off—this tailing brown finally took a Fiery Brown Beetle—the same fly it had studiously ignored during several previous presentations.

above: Prime nymph water on Nariel Creek.

With a successful assault on Little Pine tailers relying substantially on having lots of them to fish for, you can imagine how delighted Lindsay and I were to find a whole bay-full on the second evening of the trip. It was mid-week, and the lake was all but deserted, the lack of interest by other anglers compounded by a general belief that it was still too early in the season for reliable sport.

To round a point and be greeted by literally dozens of waving tails catching the gold light of sunset remains one of the most extraordinary sights I have ever seen in fly fishing. We both stood dumbstruck for a moment, not knowing where to start. Then we each identified a tail that seemed a little larger than others in the vicinity and set to work.

The next hour was as near to perfect as fly fishing gets. The trout were especially hard to fool, but with so many targets, eventually a few had to succumb. Really, it was better than if they'd been easier. Each fish hooked felt terrific because it took a lot of work to reach that moment. On the other hand, a trout bungled was not a tragedy, because there were ten more just along the shore.

When the pressure is off, it is remarkable how well you can fish, and I remember one especially large tail belonging to a trout that ignored a series of near perfect presentations. For the hell of it I whacked my Fiery Brown Beetle as hard as I could right on top of the fish. A five pounder, it abruptly up-ended and took the fly with uncustomary violence. Delighted with this response, I promptly slapped the beetle down on top of two more tailers, both of which took off with a terrified bow-wave! I laughed out loud—a luxury available only when you've already caught several nice fish.

I can't remember exactly how many trout Lindsay and I landed by the time the last tails had disappeared and we began to walk back to the car. It wasn't a huge tally, maybe half a dozen, but with all the incidental action, you'd never find two happier fly fishers.

By the time we arrived at the car the temperature had dropped from cold to freezing, and snow flurries began to drift from the clouds that raced across the gathering stars. The talk turned from the evening's fishing to the luxuries about to be offered by our warm, dry cabin just up the road at the little township of Miena. A fire, hot coffee, hot food and a hot shower. Especially a hot shower. Sometimes it's worth getting a little wet and cold on a fishing trip just to appreciate the comforts afterward.

below: Sometimes things go according to plan—Jane shows she can catch trout just as well as she can photograph them!

As we neared our lodgings, we were surprised how dark the township appeared. Even with few visitors so early in the season, we expected some lights to shine from snug windows, but they were all black.

When we opened the door of our cabin and flicked on the light switch, the mystery was solved. No power! Evidently the town had suffered a blackout. Being in the midst of Hydro Electric Commission country, pretty much all the services in the cabin—heating, stove and hot water—were reliant on electricity. A warm relaxing evening started to look unlikely. The biggest disappointment for me was the shower. I had been savouring the thought of steaming water thawing my chilled limbs for the last couple of hours. Though logic suggested this was now an empty hope, I turned the bathroom taps on just in case. As I feared, the cold tap gave an airy burp, discharged a couple of puny drops and dried up. The hot tap gave a hopeless gurgle as well, but then delivered a weak but unbroken stream of hottish water. To my delight I realised that even with the pump dead, gravity alone was sufficient to deliver the water stored in the boiler. The fact that the water had cooled somewhat since the blackout was actually fortunate, because it had reached a near perfect shower temperature.

below: A wide run on the Buckland River. Strong flows like this often make nymphing my first choice.

I somewhat selfishly declined to share my discovery with Lindsay, and got in under the shower nozzle as quickly as possible. Admittedly, the pressure didn't exactly threaten to blast me down the plug hole, but the luxurious heat almost felt better in the dark with the snow floating past the window. Not having washed since the morning of the previous

*left: A fine brown from
the edge of a swift-flowing
rapid on the Mitta River.*

right: Nymph-caught brown from the Murray, near Towong.

day, I decided to go the whole hog. I churned a decent helping of shampoo into my hair, lathered myself from head to toe in soap, and then for good measure decided on a shave and sprayed a generous layer of foam onto my chin. I did feel a little guilty about the possibility of using up all the water, but I rationalised that the power was bound to be restored soon, and anyway Lindsay hadn't seemed particularly excited about a shower.

Caked all over in various lathers, I brought the razor to my chin while simultaneously moving back under the jets to begin the blissful process of rinsing the foam from my hair and body. At that instant, the water ceased completely. There was no warning decline in the flow, just a sudden stop without a solitary drop to follow. Smeared like a cross-Channel swimmer, with a chin like Santa and hair thick with suds, I stood stranded. I didn't even have the tortuous choice of rinsing off in cold water. The freezing air I had forgotten in the steamy warmth of the shower began to return from the unheated recesses of the cabin. With no other options, I started a miserable attempt to towel off the rapidly drying soap that covered me almost to the last centimetre.

Lindsay just gaped as I slunk past to grab some clothes from my bedroom, but on hearing the explanation for my strange state he fell over laughing. Of all that day's exposed tails, the one I still hear about is my own inglorious soap-caked backside. I can't really blame him. About five years later I'm beginning to see the funny side myself.

Though hardly a hazardous pastime, fly fishing can attract injuries more serious than mere humiliation and a covering of dry soap. Spend a few thousand hours having a fly whizzing back and forth centimetres from your upper body, and it starts to become surprising if once in a while a hook doesn't decide to imbed in the said upper body. I'm lucky—I can think of only two or three times in all my fishing years that I've hooked myself. That doesn't count clothing, on which there have been a multitude of assaults, including some interesting targets like beanie balls and back zippers on fly vests. If you want to while away an hour, try removing a fly hook buried shank deep smack on the edge of zipper teeth without wrecking the zipper.

As I said though, I've got off lightly in terms of my own flesh. Except for the time I was fishing the Buckland River with Simon Gillett…

below: Peter Julian works ideal nymph water on the mighty Swampy Plains River below Khancoban.

Over a few days the two of us had fallen for a particular stretch of river that had that glorious mix of water that all fly fishers love. There are sections of the Buckland I

dislike, where hundred-metre-long greeny-black pools are separated by short rocky rapids. This beat was different, characterised by sweeping bends with gravel everywhere. Undercuts, sword grass, knee-lapping riffles two casts long, drop-offs of ideal depth, and a sprinkle of logs midstream.

It was late November and the trout were indifferent toward dries, except on evening. Weighted nymphs in size 8 were what they wanted, brown with a black wingcase, fished close to the bottom with an occasional draw. Even the shallow-water browns were uninterested unless the fly brushed the gravel. We caught our share of fish, mostly rainbows from 300 to 600 grams. The few browns we encountered were bigger, and as happens when you fish a particular stretch of water several times in short succession, we soon had a mental list of where certain elusive fish lived.

One I wanted a lot. At the bottom of an S-bend, a shallow pool spread to a broad sandy tail before accelerating down the next rapid. Just above the lip, a tangle of timber lay jammed in the middle, and on its right side a deep slot had been carved out by water turbulence. And need I say it, a brown lived there. A good fish, probably nearly twice as big as the best rainbows we had caught.

This was a nice lie, and it was no wonder that the trout had eluded us so far. Adequate presentation of a fly to its hideaway was complicated by line drag, being so near to the accelerating tail-out current, and a large expanse of shallow water over featureless flats on either side. Though the log jam provided an island of cover for the trout, the exposed surroundings seemed to make it especially jittery. Every time I approached close enough for a drag-free cast, no matter how carefully, a dark shadow would rocket upstream across the sand and disappear into the riffle above.

It was obvious by the fourth visit that a different approach was needed. Despite my general dislike of fishing downstream to trout in smooth, brightly lit water, in this case it seemed the only viable option. If I could cast horizontal to the flow from upstream of the log jam, perhaps there would be time for the nymph to drift deep and into the field of vision of the fish before drag or the mess of timber ruined the presentation.

I crept through the scrub on the left bank well back from the water, until I had passed the trout's lair by about ten metres. My backcast needed a break in the trees at right

above: My stream nymph box contains a range of bead-head nymphs, weighted nymphs and unweighted nymphs. The dries are invaders that should probably be re-organised into another box! (see Chapter 9)

angles to the river if I were to cast the required distance, and by chance there was a narrow break in just the right spot. I started to cast, half an eye following the path of the line behind as it whistled through the trees. Then as I was about to shoot forward, the trout appeared from nowhere, well up from its usual home, and took an invisible insect off the top. I should have aborted my presentation and waited, but instead I desperately changed direction mid-cast. The result was inevitable, with the backcast stuck fast two rod lengths up a springy blackwood way back in the scrub.

Cursing my luck, I watched from the shadows as the big brown swayed in bubble line mid-stream. For the first time the trout was in a comparatively fishable spot, away from the logs and the shallowest, flattest water. And it was feeding. I tugged my snagged line with violent impatience, not taking my eyes off the swaying shadow. I didn't care if the tippet broke or the fly came loose.

At a force just milligrams before the tippet ought to have snapped, the nymph pulled free of the blackwood branch and headed toward me at slingshot speed. The first I knew of this was a whack to my elbow. It didn't hurt much, but I looked down to see the fly firmly embedded right in the joint. I decided to act before I had time to dwell on my predicament, and yanked the trailing line as hard as I could, hoping to tear the fly out. Instead I drove it in deeper, and the fact that the hook point had penetrated at right angles ruled out conventional first-aid.

above: Decisions, decisions. Dad chooses a nymph for a promising riffle on the Indi River.

With the prospect of a quick and relatively painless removal of the hook gone, I sat down to consider the options. Health-wise, the best was probably a drive to the doctor at Bright for some clean surgery. However, this course was likely to rob me of several fishing hours on a day that was shaping up nicely. The better alternative, I decided reluctantly, was to have Simon cut the fly out.

I called him down from the pool above. Like a cowboy asking his faithful sidekick to dig an arrow from his arm, I mustered what I took to be a sombre, yet encouraging tone. 'Simon', I said, pointing to my elbow, 'I've buried this nymph in me halfway up the hook, and I'm afraid you're going to have to cut it out.' I waited for Simon to gasp and clutch his brow in horror. Instead he laconically remarked, 'Sure, no worries', and immediately drew his knife and began to sharpen it.

This was not entirely the response I'd been hoping for. Although I wanted my friend to show a preparedness to operate, I had imagined a little more reluctance. There was something disconcerting about the way he lovingly singed his blade with a match while chatting away happily to me.

To be fair on Simon, the operation was a success. The wound hurt like mad as he sawed away, but the hook came out quickly, and a handkerchief bandage soon staunched the bleeding. In all, the net loss of fishing time was about fifteen minutes, and we were soon back into it. But the big trout had disappeared at some point in the commotion, and for all I know he's still there now.

I have a faint scar on my elbow which Simon likes to show around after a few beers as evidence of his surgical ability. When I look at it I don't so much think of hooks and cuts, but of a dark coloured brown hanging lazily in the current above the blond sand.

right: Mark reaches for a nymph feeder.

Nymphing Mountain Rivers

Many anglers regard fly fishing on fast water like Victoria's Buckland River as being synonymous with dry fly fishing. Yet while the dry is effective for much of the season, there are periods when it will be all but useless. During times of high flow (especially spring), and to some extent during bursts of cool weather, trout will often lose interest in the surface completely and concentrate on sub-surface food. Some fly fishers make the mistake of thinking the fishing as a whole is off, when it is actually just the dry fly fishing that is failing.

When trout are not taking floating insects (and assuming there is not an emergence in progress) much of their attention will be focussed on the very narrow strip immediately above the stream bed. This almost flowless zone is where a lot of trout food—drowned terrestrials, dislodged nymphs, cased caddis—ends up. The zone also offers trout shelter from energy-sapping currents.

It is no wonder that successful mountain river nymphing often depends on getting the fly down into this zone, and keeping it there as long as possible. Heavily weighted nymphs are necessary, with a streamlined design facilitating quick sinking in the largest, fastest rivers.

In the shallower runs and riffles, where the depth is less than a metre, a sink-tip line can be helpful to get the fly down and keep it there. However, in deeper water I prefer a floating line with a long (four metre) level leader, and perhaps a split-shot or two for extra weight. Current drag on the relatively fine nylon is much less than on fly line, reducing the chance of mid-level currents bowing the line and lifting the fly up and away from the stream bed.

CHAPTER NINE

Sorting the Fly Boxes

David Dodd had just telephoned to say he'd finished my six dozen flies for the Bright trip starting the day after tomorrow. The order had been sprung on him without much notice. I tie my own flies if I have to, but only occasionally because I want to. I recognise that I don't have the aptitude, be it patience or dexterity or both, to tie flies so beautifully.

To be honest, it has never mattered that much to me whether I've caught a trout on my own creation or one tied by someone else. I can at least understand why some people find it important to tie the fly then catch the fish, or even make

above: A take on a grasshopper fly on the Kiewa River.

the rod as well. There is a nice symmetry in it. For myself, catching a trout on a fly—anyone's fly—is pleasure enough.

When David's consignment arrived I was very relieved. With the Bright trip being the first major assault on the high country this season, I was slow making the mental gear-change from lakes and lowland rivers to fast mountain streams. Not until last Friday did I realise that the furred and feathered contents of my fly boxes were dangerously low for early summer on the Ovens and Buckland. Not a single Red Tag that would pass muster, a total of two intact Royal Wulffs, all but one beadhead nymph unravelling, and so on. In short, the motley survivors of a long, sustained campaign that ended suddenly at the close of April, when attention turned again to the lakes.

David's efforts redeemed the situation. I now had a dozen Royal Wulffs (a fly I am yet to see bettered as a fastwater all-rounder), a dozen fat and not extravagantly hackled Red Tags (a first choice as a flat-water prospector), a dozen Geehi Beetles (first back-up if the preceding two don't work), a dozen Kosciuszko dun imitations (for the evening emergence that should occur at least a couple of times during the week), a dozen weighted brown nymphs, and a dozen beadheads (in case the fish aren't keen on coming to the top).

Of course there are other flies I could well use during the coming week: flying ant patterns (possibly), elk hair caddis (probably), and dainty red and orange spinners (almost certainly). I could go on. There are really no limits to what I'll try if I have to, with the emphasis on the 'if'. But at heart I am a minimalist when it comes to gear, and that includes flies. I hear the shrieks of mirth from my fishing friends, who well know that it is difficult to lift my vest with one hand. At heart, I said. Yes, I carry many hundreds of patterns in my seam-sore vest. And no, I'd rather not.

You know those periodic fly club talks, magazine articles and conversations along the lines of 'if I could only use one fly' or 'if I were restricted to half a dozen'? The author or speaker sighs and says, 'Well, if I really had to…' as if it would be pretty awful to fish under such limitations. Secretly though, I bet most of them find the idea not unattractive.

I'm like that. I know consciously that throughout any season I'll catch ninety per cent of my trout on about a dozen different patterns. Therefore, from time to time when

opposite: So many flies, which is the right one?

above: Peter Murray chooses the right fly—a Geehi Beetle —on the Corryong Creek.

faced with the big fly box sort-out, I take a deep breath and promise that some ruthless culling is about to begin. With hard expression and ice-cold intent, I tear the unused patterns from the foam ridges. Never mind that they look cute, or that they will be just the thing if I ever find trout feeding on floating praying mantis again. As the discount store spruiker says, out they go!

After about an hour of this I have created four groups of flies: the ridiculous (how did they ever find their way into the box in the first place?) bin, the untried and unused (intended for the shoe-box reserves in the study, just in case), the battle-scarred (worthy, successful but damaged flies headed for film canisters as emergency glovebox spares, or to be doled out slowly to sponging companions), and of course the pristine, proven patterns that proudly remain in the boxes. These last flies only face removal for a moment, before they are returned to tidied groupings of their siblings.

For a short time my ten fly boxes look as clean and spacious as they ever do. Each remaining fly—a Group 4 Survivor—is surrounded by such

126

an extravagant space that a cursory sweep of a given box is sufficient not only to locate a particular pattern, but a particular size of that pattern.

At about this point I begin to think that I could actually reduce the total number of boxes I carry. What if I could fit the flies from the two small Snowbee boxes into the others? This mightn't seem like much, but the Snowbees are really the ones that tip the vest over the edge from 'full' to 'overload'—the ones that create annoying lumps that dig my ribs, and cause jams when I reach hurriedly into the same pocket for another box. If you are in a hurry, a jammed box is not what you want. I attempt the shift from ten to eight and it works. Of course there is less space between each fly, but the boxes still look so tidy that less organised acquaintances will give me plenty of grief when they catch a glimpse. I'll call them jealous.

All is well, then, as I go to put the empty Snowbees back on the study shelf, I glance at the shoebox full of the untried/unused (unloved?). Uh-oh. On the right, empty fly boxes that I have managed to carry for several months, albeit with slight discomfort. On the left, at least some flies that look like they could deliver if given a chance, particularly during those unusual circumstances that crop up from time to time. I hesitate as the last of my minimalist resolve (eight fly boxes is *minimalist*, do I hear someone ask?) begins to crumble.

The pick of the extras is selected and the Snowbees are filled once more. I rationalise that although the bulk in my vest hasn't changed after all, at least the boxes are tidy.

To be fair, the unused/untried do pay their way from time to time. That weird little emerger does turn out, on a blue-winged olive Goulburn River day, to be the only fly the trout will eat. And I would never have discovered Murray Wilson's flying ant or Rick Keam's Flash Jack locust had I not made room for extra passengers when the vest was already too full. A sobering thought!

By this point in the chapter I should be offering some sort of magically neat summary. I've fly fished for the greater part of my life, so by now I should be able to come up with some memorable little rule or motto about which flies ought to be carried. If not for others, then at least for myself.

above: Some of the tools and materials a fly-tier relies upon—chicken feathers from behind the neck, called 'hackle' feathers (wound at right angles to make the bristly collar seen on many flies); a thread dispenser for applying the thread that ties most flies together; hackle pliers, for gripping the fine tip of these feathers as they are wound on; and a whip finish tool, for tying the final knot at a fly's completion.

above: The art of imitation—comparing one of Rick Keam's masterpieces with the real thing.

Sorry, I can't. I dare not restrict myself to a handful of flies, because every few years, among all the pretenders, I come across a new pattern that really does seem to make a difference. I would never have known had I not made the decision one day to put it in the 'promising but untried' box.

Even a seemingly simple and sensible decision like carrying no winter dry flies other than midges refuses to conform. At Lake Bullen Merri in July, I saw one of the biggest lake caddis hatches I've ever witnessed. It was a case of no Elk Hair Caddis, no fish. More fortuitously, a forgotten Royal Wulff in my vest wool patch caught a dozen Otway trout one early June day after all the usual wets failed. Thank goodness for Rick Keam's big foam cockchafer beetle at Treloars Bay, Cairn Curran on more than one August evening.

You might well argue that flies such as grasshopper patterns can be safely removed over winter and even spring, but will you remember to replace them before unexpectedly finding yourself at Eucumbene in January surrounded by swarms of locusts?

Perhaps I do have a philosophy on this after all. Each time you head out lugging an overcrowded fly vest, it is a little like paying premiums on an insurance policy: a drag at the time, but when the policy is actually needed, you're grateful it is there.

right: Discussing the best choice with brother Mark.

Fly Selection

Selective trout (trout feeding on one particular thing, because it is abundant and/or easy to catch) require a fly that is a reasonable imitation. But the features required to fool a trout into thinking a fly is actually 'Insect X' are often different to those required to fool an angler. Details like knee joints and wing veins in exactly the right pattern seem unimportant to trout—but how a fly sits in or on the water, and how it swims (if at all) seem to be critical distinguishing features. Get these right, and colour, size and shape only need to be approximately correct. Generally speaking, selective trout are only encountered for a small percentage of an angler's fishing time, but selective trout usually feed hard, and en masse—like the ant feeders in Chapter 2. That's why I carry so many imitative patterns in my fly box that I use so rarely.

Trout dining on a mix of prey are often referred to as 'opportunistic' feeders. A bit of a mouthful, so to speak, but a good description of the typical feeding attitude of Australian trout. They won't knock back a bit of potential prey, providing it looks and behaves in a familiar 'food-like' way. This means that flies for opportunistic trout need not necessarily copy a particular prey type. Instead, they merely have to be suggestive of food in general. Good generalist patterns, of which the Royal Wulff is a classic example, do not exactly imitate any specific species, but their behaviour and appearance are so 'buggy' that trout eat them with confidence. A good generalist pattern can often attract trout even better than a real life natural.

Favourite patterns, whether generalist or imitative, come down to an individual angler's confidence and experience, and also the type of water most frequently fished. Like favourite fishing spots, they may change over time, but most experienced anglers will have half a dozen to a dozen flies that they use ninety per cent of the time. Here are a dozen I wouldn't be without:

Bead-head Brown Nymph   *Tom Jones*   *Rick Keam Hopper*   *Foam-headed Emerger*   *Brown Nymph*   *Geehi Beetle*

Fuzzy Wuzzy   *Black Muddler*   *Barry Lodge Emerger*   *Red Tag*   *Orange Spinner*   *Royal Wulff*

CHAPTER TEN

The Devil's Grip

Jane and I live on a hilltop just over six hundred metres above sea level. Directly south, there is no higher point between us and the ocean more than a hundred kilometres distant. Nothing stands in the way of any bursts of activity that venture inland from the same cold sea that nearly killed yachtsman Tony Bullimore. Although these storms have struggled to maintain their Antarctic venom by the time they rattle our windows, and how they do rattle, it is easy to see titanic waves and cruel white foam mirrored in them.

I don't know if fly fishing has increased my fascination with weather, or if it would have been there regardless. The country has always been my home, even for the fourteen years I didn't actually live there. In the country, weather matters. A true southerly outbreak is not merely cause for remembering to wear a scarf on the walk to the morning train. It means snowfalls, power failures, trees down, and lambs dying. It also means an alpine postcard view from my window, a chance for some surreal fishing among snow on the bullrushes, and the possibility of being snowed in.

While I have mixed feelings about these strongest of cold fronts, I have none about rain. Almost always it is greeted with delight. How distant seem the glib television weatherman's apologies for rain. How shallow and cut off from the real world, where rain means life and rivers and lakes!

We didn't know it at the time, but the drought began in September 1996. The winter of that year had been unbelievably wet. It was impossible to drive across fields, even hill tops. To pull off the side of the road anywhere was to risk getting bogged. The lakes filled and spilled by the third week of August. River fishing was not generally contemplated until early summer, when persistently high, discoloured flows finally subsided.

The rain that had been falling almost daily stopped about the middle of September. We liked the stuff, sure. But with such a rainfall credit, nobody worried when it ceased

below: Autumn evening at
Lake Cairn Curran.

for a while. Sunshine, an almost forgotten novelty, was now consumed with unequivocal joy by farmers, townspeople and any anglers I encountered. By late October, the mood of a prosperous spring had not diminished in an emerald landscape jewel-studded with brimming rivers, lakes and farm dams. The only misgiving to be heard was an occasional grumble that the ground was setting like concrete.

Hardly any rain fell in November or December. Although the water credit earned over winter continued to keep the streams and water storages looking healthy, the surrounding country dried off with alarming speed. The lack of rain was compounded by an unusually hot summer. We were dismissive of long range forecasts, having seen them proved wrong so often, but by January talk of El Niño and drought was beginning to be matched by a rainfall debt that was growing with frightening speed.

The other major droughts of my lifetime, in 1967 and 1983, began abruptly and savagely. The rain simply stopped, replaced by crippling heat and scorching winds. Trees died, as did farm animals and wildlife. Bushfires of horrific size obliterated huge swathes of country. It was no surprise that the trout perished too. I remember walking with my father along the mountain creek that ran beneath our house, to a six year old as permanent as the hills and the sky, to find it dry rubble. Widely spaced pools provided evaporating sanctuary to the smallest trout, the only ones still alive. I relived the same experience sixteen summers later, walking forlornly beside neverfail Otway streams that were reduced to occasional stagnant puddles.

above: The ravages of drought —the dry bed of Lake Hume in 1998. One of our largest storages, the reservoir was reduced to just twelve per cent of capacity before the rains finally returned.

above: The Hamills Killer is a popular fly at Cairn Curran, and has a well-deserved reputation as a stillwater wet fly right across south-eastern Australia.

left: Good years on the river behind the hill. Fifteen months later, this stretch was dry except for two small pools.

A further decade and a half on, the 1997/98 drought was different, but the result was similar. It did not arrive with a lethal crash but crept upon us, hiding behind green grass, cool air and full water tanks. The reality finally struck me when I was chatting to neighbour Brian Carey, back from doing some fencing down near the river. 'Must be getting low by now,' I commented, hoping to be contradicted. It is the closest trout stream to my home, and like the Delatite of my childhood, hidden from view by a single hill. I love that little river, spring fed and a dry-summer survivor. I had left it alone this time, thinking that the trout would have enough to worry about.

'Low?' said Brian. 'Ah no, it's dry.' I didn't believe him, or at least didn't want to believe him. After all, I'd caught a flash of water through the willows when I crossed the bridge two days earlier. I went back there almost straight away. As soon as I got out of the car, I could tell he was right. The only water visible for several hundred metres was the water in the pool under the bridge. The pool itself had shrunk to the point where a single surviving trout could not hide as it darted around frantically under my sorry gaze, finding shelter only temporarily in clouds of stirred up silt.

In many places, the drought of 1997/98 will be remembered not so much for dusty, threadbare paddocks, starving livestock and bushfires, but for its toll on our waterways,

opposite: Drought on the Monaro, but the Murrumbidgee keeps flowing thanks to reliable springs and small water releases from the Tantangara Reservoir.

above: Droughts may confine fishing to the cool of after dark, in which case the Craigs Nighttime becomes a top choice of fly.

right: No drought lasts forever—Indi River, 1999.

below: Weighing up the options on a hot summer's day.

from streams and lakes through to farm dams. In our area, the scant rain that fell was well timed to provide a small sustenance ration for crops, pasture and trees, but too little for runoff, let alone the recharging of a depleted water table.

Trout are tougher than we think, and as winter began to heal the drought damage, it was a relief to find survivors where on a hot February day you wouldn't dare hope. Although most of Victoria's lakes had shrunk alarmingly, major fish kills turned out to be rare. The main effects of the drought were poor fishing, slow growth rates and damage to aquatic life, especially to the revered but fragile mayfly.

Along the streams, the damage was more marked. Some had their trout populations decimated through sheer lack of water. A lake can shrink to a fraction of its capacity and still hold enough water for trout to survive, if not thrive. A drought-struck river does not have this leeway. If the flow stops for long enough, evaporation will eventually consume all but the deepest, most shaded pools.

In too many streams, the trout were nearly annihilated. Those with good spawning facilities may recover quickly if only a small fraction of the original population has hung on to spawn after the rains have returned. In others where gravel beds are few, like my little river behind the hill, it may take years before the fishing is restored.

In eastern Victoria and the Monaro, the drought was worse. Not months, but years of inadequate rain had emaciated the country and the streams beyond belief. A long way from my home, I looked at baked ditches that I once fished, and wondered if I had dreamt the cool green water and two-kilo trout. I asked an old farmer, as dusty and withered as the surrounding land, if I could fish the river behind his house. He laughed without humour. 'You won't catch any

there son,' he said. 'The drought's sucked it dry.' As he turned to walk back inside and the flywire screen door wheezed shut, I heard him say, almost to himself, 'It's the devil's grip, you know, this drought. It's the devil's grip.'

For all its damage, the drought was not able to cast its black spell everywhere. In some places, the fishing actually thrived, even where you would least expect it. One such aberration was Lake Cairn Curran. You could reasonably assume that Cairn Curran would be ruined by a bad drought. Drier than normal years are enough to knock it around, with irrigation flows sucking it down to little more than one tenth of capacity on a few occasions over recent decades.

With the lake not even half filled by the spring rains of 1997, the prognosis for the summer and autumn irrigation season looked awful. So little 'money in the bank' seemed to guarantee a virtually dry lake before winter rains could save the situation.

Yet that is not what happened. For some reason, best known to the water supply managers, downstream water releases were unusually small and Cairn Curran did not fall below quarter full. That might still sound dismal, but even in an average year it is not unusual for the lake to fall lower, such are the huge fluctuations of an irrigation storage.

below: The sun beating down on a parched Monaro. Once again the Murrumbidgee is the only flowing water for miles.

So it was that in the middle of the drought, Cairn Curran's level was actually more stable than it had been in years. With the absence of heavy run-off, inflows were unusually clear. Instead of the water being slightly turbid, it was possible to see freshwater mussel shells lying three metres beneath the surface. This water clarity and a minimal fluctuation in level allowed weedbeds to establish to an extent rarely if ever seen on the lake. Not the usual ephemeral green carpet that forms in the shallows for a couple of months each spring, but a swaying miniature forest of mature weed, up to a metre tall. And not a choking, slimy weed, but clean individual strands that a trout could swim through without much difficulty.

In many places the weed grew in a strip lining the shore, extending out a couple of rod lengths

above: Trevor Lumb with the sort of trout that keeps us coming back to Cairn Curran —even if we don't always catch them.

and not enough to be a nuisance. In other places it formed in distinct clumps. Either way, it was ideal for fly fishing. The growth provided cover and food for the trout, while not choking the lake to the point that fishing was difficult.

An additional advantage was that the aquatic life boomed in the weed forests, and the trout achieved great condition even by Cairn Curran's high standards.

By autumn of 1998, when the summer heat had died away, Cairn Curran began to provide some fine late season sport despite the lingering drought. In a normal year the fishing would not have stood out, but after countless tough days it was wonderful to see trout feeding actively and to catch the odd one as well.

Not everyone likes this water, and I can understand that. Even among my closest fishing friends—folk you might assume to share similar fishing tastes—it would be lucky to win a secret ballot of confidence. Partly I put this down to the huge rise and fall in level. This can leave it looking fairly unattractive, with perimeter scars and lots of tree skeletons. It also throws a few people to fish a particular spot one month, and find it five metres underwater the next.

More than most waters, Cairn Curran requires faith. I was plain lucky in that my first few visits coincided with exceptional fishing. I was converted early, and my good days on the lake have been more than enough to keep me optimistic on the bad days. But if your maiden trips have coincided with smelly mudflats, turbid water and not a sign of a trout, I can appreciate your lack of regard for one of my favourite waters.

One of the things I like most about the lake is the way it often fishes well under sunny skies and light winds, rather than requiring cold grey weather for action like many of its neighbours. So it was in late season 1998. Many times I parked the car above the high-water mark and walked across the faintly green flats toward the water under a sky of crisp early winter blue. It was a rare day if my companions and I took a dozen steps without seeing the powerful swirl of a trout or two disrupting the glassy film. Maybe the fish were far out in the lake, or well down the shore, but what a boost to start the day!

It turned out that the trout were feeding on gudgeons initially, then later partaking of snails and stick caddis as well. I can only think of about two times in my life when the browns of Cairn Curran were being easy. This period wasn't one of them, but I wouldn't call them really difficult either. A slowly retrieved Tom Jones, or variation thereof, was acceptable if fished just above the weed without actually getting caught in it. Some trout were lip-hooked, some took tentatively and some came unstuck after a second or two. All this suggested the 'Tommy' was close but not perfect. We tried several other patterns, including some better imitations. These drew a complete blank, so it was back to our old reliable. Even with its shortcomings, we were still catching respectable numbers of trout. 'I think I'll leave the experimenting for another time,' said Trevor Lumb, rod bowed to a three pounder taken second cast on the Tom Jones, following an hour of no response to stick caddis and nymphs.

Eventually the drought began to break. I say began to because there was no single point when we said 'at last, it's over'. The drought slunk away slowly, quietly, and unevenly, just as it had arrived. Like a virus, it clung determinedly to some patches of country, while in others it was washed away in violent floods—the cure, in some cases, proving almost as bad as the disease.

Ironically, as green grass returned and proper stream flows were reinstated, the fishing we enjoyed at Cairn Curran actually subsided for a short while. Rising water submerged the weedbeds and discoloured inflows began to cloud the lake.

below: David Dodd tied this interesting fly that has a good reputation in rough water. On the only such day at Cairn Curran during the drought, it brought momentary promise with a take from a fish, but then failed to gather any further interest. Back to the Tom Jones!

But before this happened, there was one last day and one last evening. The shadows were long and the sun turned the sandstone ruin of an abandoned farmhouse orange. The bay that had produced two fine browns for me earlier had gone quiet for half an hour. With the evening chill descending, I considered leaving, but then a solid bow-wave creased the water ten metres beyond the weed fringe. When my false cast was still in mid-air, the fish swirled again five metres to the right. Given a clue to speed and direction I led the trout by a further five metres. The beadhead Tom Jones plopped amid the outer edge of the spreading ripple of the second swirl. I took a deep breath and let the fly settle, picturing it fluttering down through the icy water like a spent flare. When I judged it to be just above the weed fronds, I drew a slow, steady strip of line through my fingers.

Right at the end of the stroke, I felt resistance. It was ostensibly no different from snagging on weed, yet I somehow knew it was more. When the rod bent hard a second later, I could not tell you if it was caused by the draw of the trout or my lifting of the rod. The trout lunged deep at first, and the line could be felt momentarily catching the weed strands, thankfully frail enough to part without much force.

The trout turned out to be a brown of a little less than two kilos. It was amazingly strong. My surprise at its power and tenacity was lessened by many previous encounters with supercharged Cairn Curran trout, several of which had ended with an abruptly lifeless line signalling a lost chance. This time, despite head shakes, rolls, and a single leap clear of the water, the brown stayed on. It was a male, darkening just slightly in prelude

above: Trevor lays out a long cast beyond the weedbeds on one of the glorious evenings at Cairn Curran, autumn 1998.

to the coming spawning season. The water stung my fingers as I reached around the trout to free my hook. The fish was immaculate: young enough to hold superb condition in both breadth and depth, without a single scrape to a fin, but old enough to display the beginnings of a kype and humped shoulders.

It occurred to me that I was looking at this fish at the end of one of the worst droughts on record, and I was kneeling by a lake in one of the worst affected catchments. Yet a finer trout than the one in my hand would be hard to find. I fished no more that day, content to walk through the growing shadows to my car and drive homeward.

It was all but dark by the time I neared our house. On a whim, I stopped the car when I reached the river behind the hill. A cold moon lit the fields, and the still, clear sky promised frost. In the silence of a winter evening, the tinkling of the little stream sounded at once alive yet brittle. Modest autumn rains had fallen in our district and I knew that the river had been flowing for several weeks, but I felt an urge to walk its banks and see the water splashing over rock in the moonlight.

I had doubted that any trout had survived the flowless summer, yet when I rounded the bend a hundred metres above the bridge, an uneven sloshing interrupted the quiet murmur of a rare gravel-lined riffle. As I approached closer, the swirls and flashes of a pair of spawning trout were unmistakeable. The devil's grip had not claimed everything.

right: A small central highlands stream flows again, and the trout are already coming back. The drought has passed—for now.

Coping with Drought

Besides actually killing trout through taking away *all* the water, droughts threaten trout by simply *reducing* the amount of water, and exacerbating water temperature problems. The reduced depth of a lake, or flow in a river does not directly kill trout, but these circumstances make the water more prone to heating and oxygen depletion. Therefore, even though a given drought year may be no hotter than normal, water temperature is likely to be the single biggest factor in reducing trout activity, or—at worst—in trout mortality. Finding catchable trout in a drought is often a case of finding cooler water.

Tailwaters (rivers regulated by upstream reservoirs) often escape the worst effects of drought. The very purpose of many reservoirs is to guarantee a flow during the dry Australian summer, and as a bonus, the water temperature is usually chilled to ideal trout temperature by virtue of the water being released though tunnels deep beneath the lake surface.

Steep-sided lake shores dropping away into deep water allow fly-based access to trout that have taken refuge in the cooler depths, using either sinking lines, or heavily weighted flies.

During hot, dry weather, early morning is the time when the water temperature will be at its minimum, and the trout most active. Mid-afternoon is the worst time.

If the trout population in a particular river or lake is devastated by drought, recognise that recovery of the fishery may take two or three years, even if the actual habitat repairs itself quickly. An isolated population, as in a landlocked lake, will have to 'start from scratch' with the fishery not worth considering until restocked trout have grown to catchable size. But if a stream or lake is linked to a water that was unscathed by drought, like a tailwater or a deep lake, recovery through migration can be rapid.

Other Waters, Other Hills

I remember the phone call from my early guiding days. The voice on the other end introduced its owner as Gene from Missouri, USA. He was in Melbourne on business, and had three spare days. As any sensible person would, he wanted to go fly fishing. 'So the guys at the tackle shop said I didn't have to go to New Zealand, that there are trout right here. Is that for real?' So I explained to Gene that it sure was! I told him you could catch a trout an hour's drive out of Melbourne or two hours out of Sydney. I didn't even start on Tasmania. 'No kidding?' he asked. 'I thought Australia was all deserts and beaches.'

So Gene, my brother Mark and I went fishing. He was like a child at Disneyland. As we drove northwest toward the central highlands of Victoria, he stared in fascination at the big paddocks and all the sheep. I could still just see the city skyline in the rear view mirror, when he said 'This must be the Outback'. I didn't say yes, but to be honest, I didn't disagree either. We drove across the wall of a large reservoir, through tree-ferns and fifty-metre-high forest. We crossed

sparkling rivers with rocky beds. Gene had never seen them before of course, but when he said 'There would be trout in there', it was a statement, not a question.

We fished for two and a half days. I would like to say that we caught heaps. We didn't. Gene caught three, but I can still see his grin as he held the first wild brown in his hand. 'An Aussie trout', he said, almost in disbelief, 'an Aussie trout!' Sometimes we fly fishers say that 'it doesn't matter' how many we caught. Sometimes that is true, sometimes not quite. This time it was true. There was so much for Gene: koalas, kangaroos, woolsheds, gum trees. The trout were, as the cliche says, a bonus.

The only thing that troubled our guest was snakes. He was terrified of them. I have a sneaking suspicion that some mischievous bellboy or business contact had revved him up about the abundance and deadliness of Australian snakes. 'I ain't walking through them long weeds!' exclaimed Gene when we arrived at our first river. 'Well if you don't walk through the grass, we can't fish,' I observed, promising him for the umpteenth time that, as it was early November and the wind was a cold southwesterly, we would not even see a snake let alone be bitten by one.

After a nervous start, by the second day Gene was quite at home 'in the weeds'. Mark was upstream a hundred metres, scouting for rises, when he stopped dead in his tracks. 'Phil, you'd better not come up here,' he shouted, with what I immediately picked as forced nonchalance, 'There's a...ah...rare bandicoot on the bank with its young—we don't want to frighten it.' Fortunately, Gene was too preoccupied with a nearby nymphing trout to pay close attention to this charade. When we moved on, it was easy to persuade him to give the 'bandicoot' a wide berth. Having already seen a platypus and two wallabies that morning, unusual wildlife no doubt seemed commonplace. Gene said 'I guess if we scared it, it would desert its babies, right?' Once again, I didn't disagree.

I wasn't at all surprised when a little while later, out of earshot of our guest, Mark told me that the bandicoot was actually a two-metre brown snake. If you read this, Gene, our apologies! But I don't think we would have got you out of the car for the rest of the trip if you had known.

Like a lot of visitors, Gene wanted to hear all about our favourite waters, the places where the fishing is the best. I'm like that myself in new territory. When it got down to actually telling him, however, I found that things like 'favourite' and 'best' are a little hard for a fly fisher to pin down. Not because I was unwilling to give up any secrets—Gene lived on the other side of the world and was hardly likely to invade my special spots with an army of his mates. It was just that, when I stopped to think about it, it was hard to quantify streams and lakes in those terms.

Take the Monaro stream that I fished a couple of years ago. At the time it was heaven, with big trout sipping mayfly duns, but it dried up in the great drought, and has only just started to flow again. There are no trout there right now longer than my finger. How could I call it one of the best, or a favourite?

Trout water is never static. Every year is different. Wet, dry, good spawning seasons and bad. Some years the hatches are great, some years poor. Then there's the question of what makes trout water good. Do you want big fish, or lots of small ones? It is rare to have both. What if the fishing is great, but the surroundings are industrial/suburban, as on the lower Merri River? And what if the trout are tiny but the setting is breathtaking, as along the creeks draining the highest slopes of the Kosciuszko?

Do you want the trout to be easy to catch? Think about that one. And what if you could pull them out by the dozen, but you had to fish for them 'blind' because they were always holding five to ten metres down and you never saw them, except on the end of your line. Or do you want the best of the Little Pine tailers? You might see hundreds of trout within half a cast of the shoreline, yet to catch more than a couple is a minor miracle.

In the end I said to Gene, 'Look, I don't actually *know* which waters are the best, or which are my favourites. But I can tell you about some places I think are special.'

And that's what I'm going to do now, because naming a certain fishing spot as 'best' just has to be fiction. Not only does the fishing quality change almost by the week, but what constitutes 'best' is totally subjective. And even for the person doing the nominating, I'll bet the list probably changes all the time.

Some Special Fly Waters

W hen you stop and look at the area of trout country in southeastern Australia, you realise just how much exploring a fly fisher can look forward to. Even restricted to the region I will be concentrating on (from Canberra in the north to Tasmania in the south) we're talking several hundred kilometres, and who knows how many hectares, of rivers and lakes. With such a large area, and so many waters to discuss, it will help to have some maps to refer to. Those on this page give a general idea of the whereabouts of the eight districts I'll talk about, while on the following pages you will find an enlarged location guide for each district to accompany my descriptions.

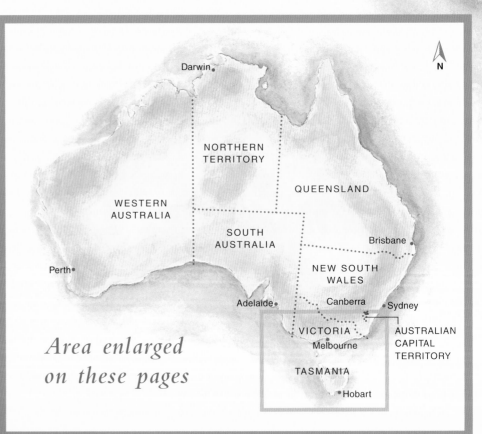

Area enlarged on these pages

left: *A glimpse of the Mitta Mitta River through the trees—one of the most important trout waters of the northeast Victoria district (page 154).*

146

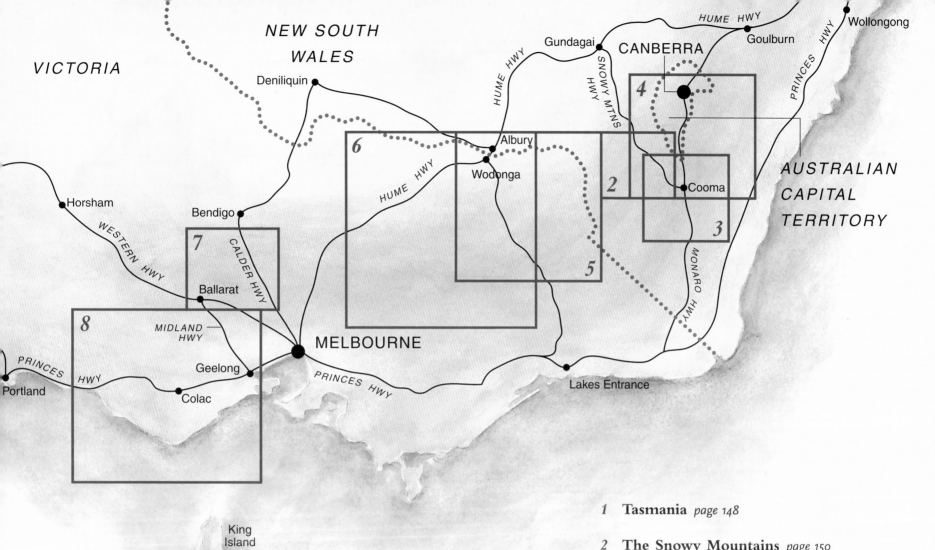

VICTORIA

NEW SOUTH WALES

AUSTRALIAN CAPITAL TERRITORY

Wollongong
Goulburn
HUME HWY
CANBERRA
Gundagai
Deniliquin
6
Albury
Wodonga
HUME HWY
Horsham
Bendigo
7
Ballarat
2
Cooma
3
PRINCES HWY
SNOWY MTNS HWY
MONARO HWY
WESTERN HWY
CALDER HWY
MIDLAND HWY
5
8
Geelong
MELBOURNE
Portland
PRINCES HWY
Colac
PRINCES HWY
Lakes Entrance

King Island

Flinders Island

1
MURCHISON HWY
Devonport
Deloraine
Launceston
Queenstown
LYELL HWY
MIDLAND HWY
TASMANIA
HOBART

TASMANIA

Where to start with Tasmania? No other Australian state comes close to offering the same sheer density of trout water. It is very difficult to find even a creek or pond that doesn't contain trout. Any attempt to list every worthwhile water here would be foolish, so I refer you to Greg French's excellent 1994 book *Tasmanian Trout Waters* and *Trout Guide* by Rob Sloane and Greg French (1991), for comprehensive coverage. I can only provide the briefest of introductory summaries.

Excellent river fishing can be found all over the island, though the major components of the Esk system—the North Esk, South Esk, Macquarie, Break O' day, and Meander rivers stand out in my mind for rising trout, dry fly fishing and the chance of a really good fish to at least a kilo. And do not assume that good fishing is reliant on the spring mayfly activity —as thrilling as this is, other quality fishing (both with wet and dry fly) may be encountered at any point in the season.

Tasmania's sea trout fishing is also superb and widespread. My brief taste of this sport centred on the storm-swept Henty River, though I know there are many other west coast estuaries considered its equal or better. Though some estuaries contain worthwhile residents all season, local wisdom suggests that the best of the true sea-trout fishing occurs in spring.

For fast flowing, wild rivers with eager and plentiful trout, the Leven, Tyenna, Liffey, Travellers Rest, Nive, Pine and upper Derwent rivers are just a tiny sample that I recall with a wistful smile. In most of the above streams, the typical trout would be a modest 200 to 400 grams, however a sprinkling of really big fish exists to raise the stakes.

It is the lake fishing that really sets Tasmania apart and elevates it to world class. It has been suggested that if Tasmania had many more lakes it would sink! Almost all but the most remote contain trout. Wild browns, and to a much smaller extent wild rainbows, have infiltrated the vast interlocking network of natural and man-made lakes that dominates the central highlands and the west coast.

If trying to pick out rivers for special mention is hard, it is even more difficult with the lakes. You know already that I enjoy Little Pine, Bronte and Dee lagoons, though they are very

TASMANIA

different waters. Lake St Clair may not have trout that are quite as large, but it is so beautiful that it can be difficult to stop gaping and start fishing. For sheer size, only Lake Eucumbene rivals the Great Lake. The scale of this water used to daunt me, as did the barren-looking shoreline. Now I enjoy the lake immensely, knowing that the huge trout population is surprisingly well spread, and relatively easy to find in the clear water with polaroids. Dee, St Clair, Bronte and the Great Lake also offer excellent evening rises and night fishing (for those who are too excited to sleep!).

Possibly the largest number of rising trout I have ever seen with a sweep of my gaze is during the summer dun hatch at Arthur's Lake—but a boat is handy to get the best of the fishing. Nearby Penstock Lagoon has fallen from favour in recent years due to turbidity. I still enjoy the shelter of its forested shores and in an autumn when the jassids (leaf hoppers) make one of their occasional appearances, the fishing here can be brilliant.

The so-called Western Lakes are too numerous to list here—there are literally hundreds, some not even named. The fishing varies dramatically from lake to lake. Some have excellent rises, while others rarely see trout on the surface. Tailers might be common in one lake, all but unknown in another close by. Probably the biggest variable is trout population, largely governed by the extent of natural recruitment. This leaves some lakes with a handful of trophies, others teeming with smallish fish. Most of the more popular lakes strike a balance between the two.

The greater part of the area is verging on wilderness, and the only section where the fisheries are easily accessible in a conventional car is the eastern edge (often informally called the 'Nineteen Lagoons' or 'Near Western Lakes'). The climate of the whole area is sub-alpine and visitors—whether travelling by car or on foot—need to be properly equipped at any time for the possibility of blizzards and white-outs.

It should be noted that despite the wilderness tag and comparative lack of fishing pressure, catch rates in this area are not especially high. However the international reputation of the region is well founded. With truly natural fisheries becoming scarcer world-wide, the Western Lakes offer anglers isolation, adventure and the chance to fish totally unspoilt waters for totally wild trout. This combined with the potential for excellent sight fishing—particularly polaroiding—is what the area is all about. You may not catch many trout on a Western Lakes trip (though on the right day even this is possible), but the overall experience is not easily forgotten.

THE SNOWY MOUNTAINS

It is no surprise that the Snowy Mountains area provides excellent trout fishing. The most elevated area in Australia provides the precipitation and the cool temperatures for idyllic trout habitat. The giant hydro-electric river diversion Snowy Mountains Scheme (SMS) has had a substantial impact on the fishery, both good and not so good. However, the enclosure of the greater part of the region within the Kosciuszko National Park is a complete success.

Lakes Eucumbene and Jindabyne are the most obvious landmarks of the SMS. I have a preference for Eucumbene, especially late summer through early autumn during good grasshopper years. Watching a kilo-plus rainbow rocket up the navy blue midday waves toward your bobbing artificial redefines the word 'anticipation'. Then there's the flooded flats in spring and if that isn't enough, the night fishing is famous. Still, I have friends who swear the Jindabyne trout are bigger. 'Just try the winter polaroiding,' they say.

The rivers in the Snowy are too numerous to mention, but three at least fit my definition of special. First, the Eucumbene River. As the major spawning tributary to the million plus trout living in the lake, no wonder it has a high head count of quality fish. I don't care for the spawn-run fishing myself, but ignoring that, the river still holds some superb residents (some of which to judge by their size are spawners that decided to stay awhile). However, crowds can make it difficult to get a nice stretch of water to yourself.

The Thredbo River, a Lake Jindabyne tributary, shares many of the characteristics of the Eucumbene. However this river is a bit bigger and a bit more inaccessible in places. If you don't mind walking and a bit of scrub-bashing, it is easier to find some privacy.

The Murrumbidgee is a quite different kind of stream. Slower and gentler, below Tantangara Reservoir it features abundant weed and huge pools—more like little lakes than part of a river. The fishing is more subtle and the country for the most part more gentle. There are fewer 'trophy trout' than in the Thredbo or Eucumbene, but the hatches are prolific and the sight fishing superb.

THE MONARO

The Monaro (pronounced 'Monairo') is a loosely defined high plain area lying east of the Snowy Mountains. For a trout fishing district it is incredibly dry, and indeed the area can suffer badly from drought for years at a time. So why list it among the special places? Because when the good years return, which will happen, the water chemistry, cool climate and topography combine to produce trout streams that rival fly fisheries anywhere in the world.

Brown trout are the mainstay of the Monaro, and in good seasons may average one to two kilos, with three kilo fish not uncommon. The condition of the trout must be seen to be believed. Even better, the sight fishing opportunities are excellent. Polaroiding is practical, and there are excellent rises through much of the season.

More than most places, the fishing varies wildly from water to water and year to year. In the right season the MacLaughlin, Kybeyan, Big Badja and Bombala Rivers can produce great fishing. The so-called creeks, especially the Campbalong, Bobundra, Rock Flat and Kydra are also gems if you hit them in a good year. I should stress that the Monaro is normally about quality fishing, not prolific fishing. It demands a fair level of skill, and though the trout may be big, they can be far from plentiful.

Perhaps this partly explains the zealousness with which many Monaro landowners guard their stream frontages. Despite the tight bag limits and catch-and-release laws now in force in the area, there are still those who flout the regulations both in letter and spirit. If you intend crossing private property to reach the water, make sure you ask first. And it won't hurt your chances if you volunteer to carefully release all your fish, even if you don't actually have to.

There is one river right on the southern edge of the district that I have a particular soft spot for: the Delegate. It isn't as famous as the others, and to be honest, it doesn't produce the same quality of trout. On the other hand, it is almost droughtproof thanks to high-rainfall headwaters, and offers a delightful variety of water ranging from huge still pools to gurgling riffles. Well worth a try.

CANBERRA DISTRICT

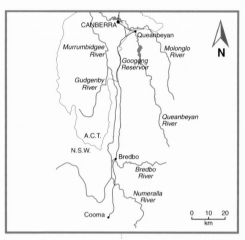

anberra fly fishers are spoilt. Not only do they have the Snowys and Monaro within day trip distance, but they have several worthy waters even closer. Googong Dam is one. Outside of high summer, this steep sided yet fertile lake offers impressive fly fishing. Large catches are uncommon, but the trout are seriously big. I've seen several in excess of three kilos, and larger fish are reported from time to time. These trout are especially keen on the resident bait-fish, and respond well to wet flies like the Hamills Killer, Mrs Simpson and, of course, the Tom Jones.

Dry fly fishing is possible, and on one drizzly November afternoon I witnessed a hatch of duns, some of which were lazily engulfed by some large trout—beyond casting range regrettably! The big fish began moving in closer as the light faded. Close enough to cast to? I never found out, because by then, we had to leave.

One disadvantage of Googong is the restricted hours of access. At the time of writing, the opening and closing times of the reserve gates effectively curtail fishing at dawn or dusk—the prime times for fly fishing. Incidentally, there was a time when Lake Burley Griffin— right in the heart of the city— was considered a viable fly option. My friend Peter Murray caught a rainbow in excess of two kilos there many years ago. As of today, though, I couldn't really recommend it.

Aside from the lakes, the district offers some great stream fishing. The Gudgenby is a small, tumbling stream in stunning mountain country. The trout aren't much bigger than the stream, but there are lots of them. Nearer to the city, the Molonglo and Queanbeyan rivers still have their problems, and some sections aren't worth bothering with due to pollution. Even so, it is worth taking the time to explore the middle and upper reaches of both: some great trout water can be found in patches. To the south, the Bredbo and Numeralla rivers aren't well regarded locally, but they have both given me hours of fun, especially during hopper season. Don't be put off by low flows and limited 'trouty' looking water. Outside of extreme drought, you can expect to find fish around any significant cover.

UPPER MURRAY

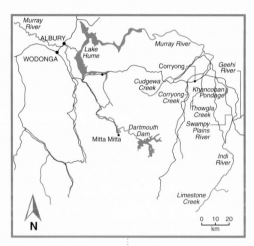

The headwaters of the Murray River separate the Snowy Mountains from the alpine ranges of Victoria. Between November and April, there are few places I would rather be. The greatest rise and fall of landscape in all of Australia can be found here. It is possible to stand among the summer snow drifts on Mount Townsend, and make out the pools and rapids on the Geehi or Swampy Plains rivers nearly two vertical kilometres below. I've talked about the upper Swampy in Chapter 2, and the Geehi is similar in history and present day fishing.

Further downstream, the valley of the Swampy broadens as it meets Khancoban Pondage—a spectacularly situated lake chilled by water tunnelled in from the higher Snowys. Below the pondage, the Swampy Plains becomes a giant tailwater. Here lie the true 'swampy plains'—of fertile green flats woven with soaks and lagoons: unlikely flat land given the surrounding towering mountains. For several kilometres the river barrels toward the Murray through sweeping gravel bends. Its blue-green water holds a fine population of trout.

Shore-based access is extremely restricted except for immediately below the pondage, so many anglers choose to raft the river.

The Murray River itself benefits greatly from the inflow of the Swampy and for many kilometres below it is kept cool enough to support an excellent fly fishery. Here is that rare combination of numbers and size. Kilo trout abound. With a good hatch of duns or a hopper plague, the dry fly fishing can be superb.

Above the Swampy Plains junction, the Murray is often called the Indi River. A more modest river without the tailwater flows, and containing smaller fish the Indi is nevertheless a delightful trout stream all the way to the headwaters. It is worth noting that the Murray and the Indi are designated as New South Wales waters, and a NSW licence is needed even if casting from the Victorian bank.

Smaller tributaries of the system: the Limestone, Thowgla, Corryong (Nariel) and Cudgewa creeks should not be ignored, and these waters can provide great dry fly fishing through the warmer months.

NORTHEAST VICTORIA

There is no obvious geographic boundary between this region and the upper Murray, and I often group them together. The nature of the rivers, the breathtaking mountain scenery and the style of fishing continues. The largest river in the district is the Mitta. From the cold tailwaters below Dartmouth Dam, to the wild and largely forested reaches

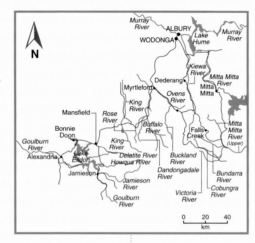

above, this river is one of Victoria's most impressive trout streams. Its major tributaries, the Cobungra, Bundarra, Victoria, Gibbo, and Middle Creek are each significant trout waters in their own right. Visitors should note that all feature extensive stretches in wild country that are difficult to reach, though road access does exist.

A mountain range away from the Mitta flows the Kiewa. Though its east and west branches offer some fishing, the main stream is the feature water for the fly. The surrounding mountains are rugged, inaccessible and heavily timbered, but access along the roadsides and via bridges on the cleared valley floor is very good, offering tens of kilometres of excellent water for fly fishing.

The next major valley west belongs to the Ovens. In a similar setting to the Kiewa and again offering extensive access, the Ovens arguably ranks slightly lower because it does not fare as well during droughts or dry summers. The major tributaries of this system, the Buckland, Buffalo, Dandongadale and Rose, all flow down from more rugged country. Access is reasonable nevertheless, and all frequently offer very good fly fishing.

The King is strictly an Ovens River tributary, but it joins the larger stream well beyond the downstream limits of trout habitat. Many regard the upper reaches of the King above Lake William Hovell, as the finest natural trout stream in Victoria. I'd be reluctant to go that far, but it is certainly a superb stretch of river both scenically and for fly fishing, all the more protected by limited, arduous access.

Finally we come to the streams feeding Lake Eildon. These were my earliest 'home waters', and I remain fond of them today: the Jamieson, Howqua, Delatite and Goulburn. The Goulburn below Eildon is a justifiably famous tailwater.

VICTORIAN CENTRAL HIGHLANDS

Between Woodend and Ballarat, and running for 50 kilometres or so either side of the Great Dividing Range is the area I loosely describe as the central highlands. Ranging from roughly 400 to 800 metres above sea level, it is not a world-class fishery, though you know you are in trout country when good fly fishing exists at Lake Wendouree in the heart of the area's largest city, Ballarat. Still, this region surrounds my home so naturally I have a fondness for many of the trout waters in the area.

There are some small rivers and creeks in the area that contain trout, and a run of several wet years can produce good, if demanding, fly fishing. However the lakes are the mainstay of the district, providing some of the most reliable trout fishing within daytrip distance of Melbourne. Through good years and bad, Newlyn Reservoir, Hepburn Lagoon, and Harcourt Reservoir, continue to produce worthwhile fly fishing. Catches are seldom high, but the size is good: each water produces plenty of one kilo trout each season, and much larger fish are taken. These lakes, together with Wendouree, have particularly good mayfly populations and the dun hatches through October and November (earlier at Harcourt) can be superb. Look for action in the early afternoon on overcast days.

A little further east are the Upper Coliban Reservoir, Lauriston Reservoir and Malmsbury Reservoir which do not have the same level of mayfly activity (though it can still be significant). This is made up for by superior margin fishing in late winter/ early spring, as lake levels and a better response from the trout during the warmer months to terrestrials such as beetles, grasshoppers and ants.

At the northern extremity of the district, Cairn Curran Reservoir is one water that I have a particular affection for, though as I say in Chapter 10, this lake is not for everyone. Among its extensive range of fly fishing opportunities, Cairn Curran may be best known to fly fishers for its smelters— trout chasing small minnow-like fish. This activity is also an early and late season feature of many of the other lakes mentioned, with late autumn the peak time.

SOUTHWEST VICTORIA

Having declared a sentimental attachment for the previous area, I must do the same for the southwest of the state. Through my teens it provided the closest trout water to my home south of Geelong. It remains a favoured area for me today. The nature of the fishing in the southwest varies enormously.

On the one hand are the tumbling rainforest creeks of the Otway Ranges. Every permanent stream crossed by the Great Ocean Road, or the Cape Otway Road inland, contains a population of wild brown trout—mostly small, but keen risers. A box of Red Tags and Royal Wulffs, a good pair of wading boots, and a willingness to walk upstream for a few hours is likely to produce plenty of sport (though little of size) from November to April.

In contrast are the large, super-fertile stillwaters of the inland volcanic plain—in particular lakes Purrumbete, Modewarre and Murdeduke. There are few trees, the countryside is flat and windswept, and the trout are anything but small—four kilo fish are a regular capture at each lake, though the visiting fly fisher should expect trout to average

one to two kilos. These fish rise to insects infrequently, but often disturb the surface while smelting. Smelters provide the best chance of sight fishing on all three lakes. Unlike the Otways, regular action is improbable, and the southwest lake fisher should be prepared to put in many hours for a chance at one of these much larger trout. Summer fishing here is often compromised by excessive water temperatures, so a visit is best scheduled for the cooler months. Before we leave the lakes I should mention a water called Bullen Merri. Present problems mean it is troutless, but all fly fishers hope it will soon recover to its former status as a trophy rainbow water.

Fitting neatly between the stillwaters and the Otway creeks are the substantial rivers of the district: the Aire, Gellibrand, Merri, Hopkins, and Barwon rivers, and the Mount Emu Creek. The first three have trout in their upper reaches, but are most famous for the excellent sea-run and estuary trout fishing in their lower sections. The second three are best fished in their middle reaches, where large pools linked by short rapids offer browns averaging a kilo.

FURTHER FIELDS

Some people are going to read this and say 'hey, he hasn't mentioned the such and such, my favourite water'. There are a few possible reasons for this. The first is that I simply haven't been there so I can't comment. A second reason may be that while I have visited briefly, the experience was too short, and my overall knowledge of the place too patchy, to make a meaningful comment. A third possibliity is that the place in question doesn't rate as special to me. That's just my view. Remember because one fly fisher regards a water as average, doesn't mean another won't love it. Look at me and Lake Cairn Curran. Besides, 'not special' in this context is not synonymous with 'bad'. There are a lot of waters that I haven't mentioned which I am more than happy to fish, but for various reasons—many unashamedly subjective—they didn't make the cut. With hundreds and hundreds of trout waters in Australia, I had to draw the line somewhere!

Some rivers and lakes I'm sure I'd like if I visited them. Simon tried to get me to come over to South Australia several times when he lived there. 'I've found some great little creeks, but I can't tell you their names,' he'd whisper down the phone as if it were being bugged. Lindsay rings me every second week with his stories about the lakes and streams of central New South Wales. Oberon Dam, Lake Lyell, Lake Wallace, Macquarie River, Turon River, Duckmaloi River, and—true title—the Fish River. He seems to get some nice trout out of all of them. I haven't been there for a cast as yet but maybe I will have made their acquaintance by the time you read this.

Or ventured further northeast to the rainbow-dominated waters of New England, from Walcha north to Glen Innes and east to Dorrigo. My good friend Rick Keam has many a story to tell about this area. 'Time you went there for a few days, Phil,' he often says. 'It's only a fourteen hour drive from your place.' This he adds in a tone that suggests such a distance to prime water should be no obstacle to any fly fisher worthy of his vest!

One area that even Rick might concede is a long way away (about 4,000 kilometres in fact) is the southwest of Western Australia. While I have fished there briefly, the time was too short for a meaningful assessment. Still, my WA contacts are quite capable of giving a drool-worthy fly fishing report. From what little I know of the Blackwood River, Collie River and Warren River to name a few, I believe them.

Glossary

Blind fishing ('fishing blind'): Fishing the water without actually being able to see trout, or signs of trout.

Bubble line: A narrow strip at the centre of a river's current, lined with bubbles from broken water upstream.

Caddis: Adult insect somewhat resembling a small moth. Larval and pupal stages live beneath the water, often inside a manufactured or adopted case.

Dry fly ('dry'): An artificial fly that floats.

Dun: The drab-coloured form a mayfly takes immediately after it emerges from its nymphal shell in the surface film.

Emerger: An insect in the process of changing from its aquatic phase to the adult flying phase.

Fly line: Plastic or polymer coated line that gives fly fishers the weight they need to cast. Often designed to float.

Leader: Length of monofilament nylon separating fly line from fly: tapered, and generally three to four metres long.

Mayfly: Northern Hemisphere common name, continued in the Southern Hemisphere, for a group of insects spending most of their lives beneath the water as nymphs then emerging as flying insects. Within a few days (even hours) of emergence, mayflies mate and die.

Nymph: Broad term used to describe the juvenile phase of aquatic and other insect species. Also a generic term for a category of artificial fly.

Nymphing: Fishing with an artificial nymph.

Opportunistic: A kind of feeding behaviour described at length in notes to Chapter 9.

Pattern: Synonym for 'fly'. Alternatively, the recipe for a particular type of fly.

Polaroiding: Searching for trout with polarising glasses.

Riffle: Shallow, broken water flowing swiftly over gravel.

Rise: The act of a trout taking an insect off the water's surface; or, the disturbance left by a trout taking an insect off the water's surface; or, a number of trout taking large numbers of insects on or near the surface.

Selective: A kind of feeding behaviour described at length in notes to Chapter 9.

Sight fishing: Looking for individual trout, or disturbances made by trout, before casting.

Smelter: Trout chasing schools of small fish, one species of which is often the Australian Smelt.

Spawner: Trout on annual breeding migration.

Spinner: Final phase in a mayfly's life. The dun phase sheds another skin to become a spinner, often revealing a shiny and colourful insect.

Strike: Lifting the rod to set the hook once a trout has taken the fly.

Take: A trout eating the fly.

Terrestrial: In fly fishing, often a word used to distinguish land-based insects (like beetles and ants) from those insects with an aquatic phase in their lifecycle (like dragonflies and mayflies).

Tippet: Final metre or so of a leader to which the fly is tied.

Wet fly ('wet'): An artificial fly that sinks.

Index